HINDUSTAN
UNDER FREE LANCES
1770-1820

HINDUSTAN UNDER FREE LANCES

1770-1820

SKETCHES OF MILITARY ADVENTURE IN HINDUSTAN DURING THE PERIOD IMMEDIATELY PRECEDING BRITISH OCCUPATION

BY

H. G. KEENE

RICHARD TEMPLE

GYAN

Published by

GYAN

Gyan Publishing House
5, Ansari Road
Daryaganj, New Delhi-110002
Phone: 011-47034999, 9811692060
E-mail: books@gyanbooks.com

Distribution Network
gyanbooks.com
India, USA, Canada, UK, Australia

ISBN: 978-93-6280-201-9 (HB)
First Published, 1907

2nd Impression 2024

Printed at: Gyan Press, Delhi.

HINDUSTAN UNDER FREE LANCES 1770-1820
Author: H. G. KEENE, RICHARD TEMPLE

HINDUSTAN
UNDER FREE LANCES

THE BEGUM SOMBRE

DIED 1836.

HINDUSTAN UNDER FREE LANCES

1770–1820

SKETCHES OF MILITARY ADVENTURE IN HINDUSTAN DURING THE PERIOD IMMEDIATELY PRECEDING BRITISH OCCUPATION

BY

H. G. KEENE, C.I.E., HON. M.A., OXON.

FELLOW OF CALCUTTA UNIVERSITY, AUTHOR OF "SINDHIA" IN "RULERS OF INDIA," "HISTORY OF INDIA," "THE FALL OF THE MOGHAL EMPIRE," AND OTHER WORKS

WITH A PREFACE BY THE LATE

RT. HON. SIR RICHARD TEMPLE, BART., ETC., ETC.

(*Sometime Governor of Bombay*)

WITH ILLUSTRATIONS

LONDON

BROWN, LANGHAM AND CO. LTD.

78 NEW BOND STREET W.

1907

To

FIELD-MARSHAL THE EARL ROBERTS, V.C.,
ETC., ETC.

MY LORD,

The opinion on the first draft of this work which you were good enough to express has emboldened me to ask permission to inscribe this page with your honoured name.

I am, respectfully yours,

THE AUTHOR.

PUBLISHERS' NOTE

THE chapters in this book originally appeared in the *Calcutta Review*, and at the request of many readers the work was published in book form in Calcutta in 1901 (on account of the author) under the title of *The Great Anarchy*. The author, dissatisfied with the form in which the volume was issued, cancelled the publication after the subscribers' copies had been distributed. This new and revised edition has been prepared for circulation in this country, and the title has been changed to one more indicative of the contents of the volume.

PREFACE

I HAVE been asked by Mr. Henry George Keene, with whom I have an almost lifelong friendship, to write a brief preface to this work of his. The title of the book is *The Great Anarchy*, and the narrative depicts the situation of India just before the British acquired power. The words "Darkness before Dawn" have been applied to heathenism before the rise of Christianity. They may also have a political significance, and in that sense they possess a wondrous applicability to the condition of India during the course of the eighteenth century before the Imperial control introduced by the British soon after its close. Never in the chequered history of all the ages had India known such an anarchy as that which then prevailed. When I landed in India about the middle of the nineteenth century, no witnesses survived to attest the horrors and miseries of that time, but the children or at least the grandchildren of the sufferers were still present to recount the testimony handed down to them by their parents.[1] Thus an immense volume of tradition remained in the fullest force. Mr. Keene himself resided and exercised authority for many years in the tracts and regions most severely affected by the calamities and visitations. I also had a similar experience, and perhaps had even wider opportunities for measuring the enormous dimensions of this widespread destruction. The Moghal

[1] The writer of the following chapters twice conversed with actual survivors: a jemadar of Geo. Thomas's service and a man who had been in the "Gosain" brigade of Himmat Bahadur in 1785.—H. G. K.

invasion of Central Asia in the Middle Ages has been likened to a shipwreck of the nations. A similar catastrophe overtook some of the noblest nationalities of India 150 years ago. Nothing but the strong arm of British power could have raised them from this "slough of despond." The area thus submerged by this inundation of misfortune comprised the Northern, the Central, and the Western parts of India. It was not much less than a million of square miles, and must have contained over one hundred millions of people, all unhappy and troubled in a greater or lesser degree. With the whole of this area I have been in one way or another officially connected, and have met the immediate descendants of those who were concerned in the affairs of that troublous era. Thus having personal knowledge of these regions and their several nationalities, I am qualified to explain the merits of Mr. Keene's present work.

He is himself extraordinarily capable of unravelling the skeins of this complex subject, in which personalities and nationalities, diversities and contrarieties are combined and confused. Yet out of all this confusion he evolves a narrative, lucid and succinct, so that the reader who may desire to follow the romantic fortunes of any individual, or family, or political party, can do so with ease. Indeed, when undertaking to deal with this subject he approached it with a mass of preparatory and collateral information gathered through many years of study—a study, too, conducted often on the very scenes of the events. His first considerable work was entitled *The Fall of the Moghal Empire*, a theme demanding the powers of an epic poet, had such a one arisen in Asia. This event, vitally affecting what was then, next after China, the finest part of Asia, began to come about in the days when the crown of England descended from King William to Queen Anne and when the star of Marlborough was in the ascendant. The descent once set in motion proceeded with the rapidity with which a mass of rock rolls down a precipice to the abyss beneath. So the story of this series of events, tending under the direction of Providence to one and the same fatal result, was graphically told by Mr. Keene in his first book. This was followed by his other work, entitled *A Sketch of the History of Hindustan*, relating to a region which formed an important section in the vast theatre of disturbance, though it did not comprise the whole. Then came his monograph on Sindhia, the only one of the Maratha rulers who tried to educe order out of the chaos of anarchy. Thus armed with learning and with something more than that, namely, the knowledge gained by residence on the spot or by contact with the descendants of the very actors in the historic tragedies, Mr. Keene essays his task in a manner that no other living writer could display.

Such a narrative will naturally embrace the movements of Native Indian princes, rulers, rebels, upstarts, and brigands whenever their brigandage was on a scale large enough to require mention, which it but too often was. But in the narrative there is another element, and that a most peculiar one, which will perhaps have more interest for the English reader than the purely Native Indian parts of the story; and the element is in this wise. An English reader, who though possessing general culture might not have followed the details of Asiatic warfare and disturbance, would probably be surprised to hear that, in the anarchy which followed the downfall of "The Great Moghal" and prepared the way for British rule, European adventurers outside the control of any European Government, British or other, were among the main factors. These Europeans, more of continental than of British stock, were like stormy petrels hovering over the sea of trouble, or like mariners in their barques riding on the crests of the waves, often nearing the breakers, yet rarely striking on them and but seldom engulfed. Often they directed the political storms, and sometimes they even guided the whirlwinds. Their origin was as various as their employments: Italians, Savoyards, French, Flemish, Dutch, and occasionally even British; some were of gentle, almost noble birth, some were soldiers from the ranks, some were from the forecastle, some were deserters, some were mere swash-bucklers, some were gentlemen and administrators, some were honourable though rough soldiers, some were mere money-makers, and some were adventurers of the meanest type. Many, perhaps most of them were French. Before the French Revolution, say 1790, they were of good birth; after that they were of a very inferior class.

Asiatic rulers have always been glad to obtain the services of Europeans so long as these continued to be servants, and it is only when such a servant begins to be masterful that jealousy arises, either on the part of the ruler or his Asiatic servants. Besides this general motive, there was a special motive for employing Europeans when political existence was always a struggle for life and death on the part of all Native Indians who had to keep their heads above the seething surface of political whirlpools. Then it was that they must have at any cost men who could drill troops in camp and lead them in the field. Doubtless when such men rose to high commands, having organised their Asiatic battalions for victory, and then were entrusted with high civil authority, then, no doubt, their Asiatic fellow-servants must have been jealous, and such jealousy must have been dangerous, involving among other risks the chances of assassination. Still, in the main they were so useful as to be quite the necessary men to their employers under the stress of emergency. But there was yet another reason for their employment. The infant Colossus of British power was already showing itself in several quarters. Its growth was precarious; still, growth there always was, often depressed, but never stamped out, ever springing forward again after temporary retrocession. There was about it a vitality, a spring, a verve, a motive force, a steadiness and stability which simply struck terror into the minds and hearts of every Asiatic, high and low. Its qualities were so alien to anything known in Oriental experience, that all India lay under the dread, like that of a nightmare, that the British, if so minded, might attain to universal mastery. Of this masterful ambition and of this persevering temper the signs were everywhere apparent. It immediately occurred to every Indian who cut his path to power, or waded through blood to the seat of temporary authority, that his best chance of saving himself from the advancing British was to employ some man or men of the fateful European races. A man of British nationality would not be suitable, because presumably he could not be trusted to oppose his own people. Moreover, he would not be obtainable, because, if really an able man, he could find employment under his own Government. Thus the men available would be of continental origin. It was thought that even if they were not as effective as the English, they were at all events white men with a good share of the capacity which always distinguishes Europeans. Some were chosen either in reference to credentials or to known antecedents; others, again, were employed first in some humble capacity and then raised themselves higher by sheer prowess. Several of them won victories or other military advantages for their chiefs. All of them without exception were rewarded with a richness astonishing even to Anglo-Indians. Some of them amassed really immense fortunes in reference to the nature of their work and to the circumstances of their epoch. Indeed, the amounts and sums of wealth would at first sight seem unaccountable when it is remembered that at this time India was agitated from end to end, her social life being shaken to its very foundations. It is, however, to be remembered that, despite all superficial appearances to the contrary, the accumulated wealth of

India has at all times been enormous. Casual observers may be tempted to suppose otherwise, but those whose gaze can penetrate to the bottom well know that with an abounding population of thrifty habits, addicted generally if not universally to save and spare, to accumulate and to secrete, there will always be resources amassed in a smaller or greater degree according to the ability of the individual. Consequently at this dark era—that is to say, in the second half of the eighteenth century—there were incalculable quantities of stored and hoarded possessions. Therefore it is that in a brief time these European soldiers of fortune acquired that wealth that would have appeared to them fabulous before they entered the Oriental service, and must have transcended any visions that may have haunted their ambitious dreams. Some of them were not content with Native Indian subordinates, but employed Europeans in lesser, even humble, capacities. Such men, of course, merged into obscurity, while the names of their leaders remained conspicuous. Thus the number of Europeans great and small in Native Indian service was at certain times and in certain places quite appreciable. On the whole it may be said that in the contests which were going on at this era, running sometimes crosswise, at other times parallel, to one another, and oftentimes overlapping each other, the Europeans in native employ did in some degree mould events and almost directed the stategy of conflicting forces. Their system of drill and discipline was generally adopted, especially in the artillery and infantry, and where it was not adopted, particularly in the cavalry which was usually irregular, the results were disastrous. One of the great authorities of the time is understood to have pronounced that the Native Indian princes would have fared better had they never made use of the alien aid of the Europeans. It is difficult to say whether any such dictum could be affirmed or not, inasmuch as the Native States, which then comprised three-fourths of

India, were foredoomed to subjugation by the British power, whatever they might do or not do. But this much may be affirmed, that owing to the European officers in the Native States the rising floods and streams of anarchy were diverted in directions where they would not otherwise have flowed. Moreover, when at the beginning of the nineteenth century the British came to close quarters with the Native States, the influence of these European officers had abated and their numbers had decreased. Nevertheless the drill and discipline which they had introduced still remained and caused the native resistance to the British forces to be stiffer than it would otherwise have been on several well-fought fields.

It may be well for a moment to dwell on the character of the area, the field and theatre of action, in which these European adventurers, under their Native Indian chiefs and sovereigns, fought, conquered, conducted or endured sieges, and managed provinces during the eighteenth century. These lands are indeed some of the most classic and historic in the East, and upon each one of them these white soldiers of fortune had left the mark of European handiwork, although serving under Native Indian *régime*, before British authority came to comprehend the whole country with its all-embracing control. Such a summary survey of this historical geography can be immediately had from a glance at the map.

Let a beginning be made from about midway in the north of India, midway also in the southern base of the long Himalayan mountain range; that is to say in Hindustan, or the upper basin of the Ganges and its affluent the Jumna; ever the principal seat of Empire in India, a uniquely Imperial province; politically the most important part of the whole country. In it are the twin capitals of Dehli and Agra; and around Dehli in particular are laid some of the most striking scenes in Mr. Keene's drama of the Great Anarchy. Then let us, advancing due south, in imagination cross first the Ganges, then the Jumna. So we pass by Ujain, with its ruins of hoar antiquity, then by Gwalior, the rock-citadel destined to become the seat of the one power that stayed the course of the Great Anarchy, and by Rajputāna, bordering the Western Desert of India, that after severe struggles barely escaped submergence under the flood of almost universal revolution. Next let us, still proceeding southwards, march into the very heart of Central India, crossing the Vindhya range and the broad uplands and undulations connected therewith, right down to the north bank of the Narbada, point after point in which is signalised by some event in Mr. Keene's story. Crossing this, the queen of beauty among Indian rivers, we must on our historic tour, ever advancing southwards, ascend the Sautpura range, the true backbone of the Indian continent, descend into the valley of the Tapti river, and so reach the northern uplands of the Deccan, marked by the remains of nationalities many centuries old and by the comparatively modern associations of the Great Anarchy. So we arrive at the Deccan, the southern plateau of the Indian continent, second only to Hindustan in importance amidst the mediæval revolutions and in the more recent politics of India. For Mr. Keene's story the Deccan must be divided into two distinct spheres of action, one the Deccan of the Hindu Marathas, with its capital at Poona, the other the Deccan of the Moghals, or the Moslem Nizams, with its capital at Haidarabad. Now this line of imaginative march has extended over full a thousand miles. Outside the regions thus compassed there are no doubt provinces in the north-west, the east, the south. Still within it are most of the dominant places in India, most of the localities best deserving the attention of the student who desires to understand the miserable condition of the heritage which fell into the hands of the British at the beginning of the nineteenth century; the vineyard which, having been broken down, torn up and trampled under the iron heel, had to be restored to order by British conquest, and set up again by Western administration. Indeed, a practical apprehension of the geography above sketched is most desirable, if not absolutely essential, to the appreciation of Mr. Keene's narrative.

In a preface like this it is impossible even to mention these numerous European adventurers. The reader who may be curious to follow their careers will gladly refer to Mr. Keene's pages. The life of each one among them is strange and peculiar; indeed, very uncommon even for a land like India, which is ever fertile in wonders. Each career is full of instruction to every student who wishes to observe human capacity and individual possibilities under abnormal conditions. Among the most remarkable of these cases will be found that of M. Boigne, a Savoyard by birth, education, and experience, who rose to be the right-hand man of Sindhia, the most potent native chief then in India, and ultimately retired to his native Savoy, dying there in wealth and honour; that of Perron, a deserter from the French Navy, a common man, who, by his mother-wit, became the military successor of Boigne, was taken prisoner of war by the British General, Lord Lake, and after release, died obscurely in France; that of George Thomas, a deserter from the British Navy, an unlettered man with some genius, who contrived to establish an almost independent dominion in parts of Northern India, but had ultimately to surrender himself to British authorities in whose custody he died on his way to Calcutta. The effect of these and all the other careers can be gathered only by a perusal of Mr. Keene's book.

In this brief summary justice cannot be done to Mr. Keene's historical style, which has a masterly grasp of details and arrays them with truly pictorial effect. To the general reader just a few passages may be specially commended as examples illustrating the romance of

Indian life during the eighteenth century; though, indeed, the whole history is like an epic poem, save that the composition has the living force derivable only from reality and truth. For facility of reference the numbers of the chapters are given from which the examples are taken. The passages may be designated as the capture by the British of Law (nephew of the notorious speculator), the Franco-Scot who was fighting on the Native Indian side against his own countrymen (Chap. II.); the narrow escape of Boigne from assassination (Chap. IV.); the headlong charge of Rājput chivalry, and their return through a Valley of Death, four thousand saddles emptied by the fire of regular infantry (Chap. IV.); the rescue of the Emperor of Dehli from imminent death by the Sardhana troops (Chap. VIII.); the superb charge of the heavy-armed cavalry of Rajputāna upon Du Drenec's regulars (Chap. VII.); the Muslim defeat at Kardla, and the memory of Raymond, to this day cherished at Haidarabad as that of the *preux chevalier* (Chap. VII.); the fateful flight of the princess Begum Sombre, her attempted suicide with an ineffectual stiletto, and the simultaneous self-destruction of her husband by a pistol-shot; the last struggles and final surrender of George Thomas (Chap. VIII.); the capture of Perron by Lord Lake (Chap. XI.); the bloody and hard-fought battle between the Maratha chiefs when the troops on both sides were led by European officers, and when indeed Greek did meet Greek (Chap. XI.); Skinner and his "yellow" regiment of horse at the siege of Bhurtpur, the dam being seized by the besiegers in the nick of time, preventing the besieged from flooding their moat (Chap. XII.); Gardner drawing his sword upon his Native Indian sovereign when provoked by insult in open Durbar or Levee (Chap. XIV.).

These striking scenes are but specimens of the great *repertoire* of historic scenery which Mr. Keene's narrative comprises, and of the picture-gallery it contains.

Near the end of the book, in Chapter XV., doubts are apparently expressed regarding the internal policy of Dalhousie and Lawrence, though their political virtues are acknowledged. As they are statesmen of a school to which I have been proud to belong, these doubts naturally are not shared by me. Some questions, too, are raised regarding some branches of recent British administration, such as education, sanitation, and the like; here also I am unable to concur, while I admit, on the other hand, that these subjects are all the better for free discussion.

This, however, in nowise hinders me from giving the most cordial adhesion to the historic truths and the political principles most ably and effectively set forth in the main and the essential portions of this work.

RICHARD TEMPLE.

INTRODUCTION

THERE is some danger of the Indian Empire being too much taken for granted in the daily cares of our national life. It is easy to forget what a mighty task we have undertaken there; and that the introduction of British power was an essential stage in the social evolution of the various races who people that vast and varied region. At the dawn of the nineteenth century all seemed dark; the stars were paling and it was not by any means plain what the day was likely to be. None the less, because quite unconsciously, was it preceded and prepared by the labours of individual Europeans, who served competing native chieftains, and set up a standard of order, preparing men's minds for some vague ideas of discipline and duty. [See Colonel Malleson's opinion; also citation from *Bengal Journal* of 1790, *ap.* the present writer's *Sindhia*, p. 180.]

Some notion of these men and of their work is helpful in recognising the need for intelligent leading in such conditions. It is here offered, as found in contemporary records; including letters from General de Boigne and others. The chapters appeared originally in the *Calcutta Review*, and the author has to thank the Editor and Proprietors of that serial for permission to reproduce them in the present form. The letters of which mention is made above have never before been published: for the use of them thanks are due to Mr. S. Sutherland. Information as to Perron has been courteously communicated by one of his descendants, Colonel the Marquis de Brantes.

This little book was not undertaken in any spirit of controversy. But there are mistakes made about British India ; and the writer will not deny that he would gladly think that it was in his power to give them any correction. Many, both in India and in England, believe in a splendid past to which the people are debarred the return by an alien dominion. Any knowledge of the facts will be beneficial by which such persons can be disabused. The Moghal Empire of India fell in pieces in the eighteenth century A.D., the first blow being given in 1757, when Clive beat the Moghal Viceroy at Plassy and placed a vassal of the East India Company on the seat of administration—the *musnud* of Bengal. The Great Anarchy deepened while Afghan and Maratha contended for power in Hindustan ; a beginning was made of its extinction when Lake took Dehli in 1803. There are, therefore, exactly fifty years of almost unrecorded darkness to be dealt with ; and some attempt to deal with it will be found in works mentioned on the title-page, and in the pages which follow.

The scope of the present work imposes strict limitations ; and the general history of the Moghal Empire in India stands on record in easily accessible works. It will suffice here that the reader should be reminded of the close resemblance of the case to that of the Roman Empire in the time of Septimius Severus. Like that monarch, the celebrated Alamgir—better known by his title of Aurangzeb—had obtained the throne by treachery and murder, and was compelled to dependence on extensive military action for his maintenance in power. After an administration of indefatigable ability, energy and industry, Aurangzeb died on a remote and difficult enterprise, and the decline of the Empire almost instantly began. The intrigues of politicians, the growth of insubordination, the rapid succession of incompetent sovereigns, precipitated the disintegration of the Empire, until foreign invasion from various quarters rendered recovery impossible. After a period of some twelve years, during which there was not even a titular Emperor at Dehli, the wandering heir obtained a sort of restoration in 1771. But he was a complete dependent, at first of the Marathas, afterwards of a Persian Minister, until 1788, when he was blinded by a Muslim adventurer, and afterwards held in honourable confinement by Sindhia and his European subordinates until they were driven out by the British in 1803. It is during this miserable "reign" that the Great Anarchy became complete in Hindustan.

In the transliteration of native names the system originated by Sir William Jones has been generally followed, vowels having the same value as in Italian. Exception, however, has been made in respect of a few words like Calcutta and Lucknow, which have become naturalised in our language.

The state of Hindustan and parts of the Deccan during the latter years of the eighteenth century was one of the most terrible ever beheld in a country with any claim to civilisation. Every province had fallen away from the Imperial throne; some to become independent under usurping satraps, others to pass, like Bengal and the Carnatic, into the power of intrusive aliens. Into these latter peace and a sort of awkward administration were entering; elsewhere the land was full of the smoke of burning homesteads, and the reek of innocent blood. Every man, wrote an eye-witness, lived as in a forest of wild beasts, and owed his safety only to the strength of his own heart and arm. Over and above the miserable villagers by whom, in spite of all, the earth continued to be a little cultivated, there were, in each great denomination, two classes of ruling men possessed of what, by comparison, might be called education. Among the Hindus were the Brahmans, remotely descended from Aryan forefathers and still retaining some signs of superiority in body and mind; while the leaders of Muslim opinion were the Moulvis, claiming descent from Arabian Shaikhs and Sayyids. The military members of either creed were twofold: the Rājputs and Marathas on one side, the Moghals and Pathans on the other. Among these six raged a deadly enmity, each apparently aiming at the extirpation of the other.

In such a state of things a great prize appeared before the minds of able and ambitious leaders: and any advantage that would enable a man to overthrow all opposition was eagerly sought for. Such an advantage seemed within the reach of Sindhia when he first observed "with what majesty the British soldier fights." If he could obtain the services of a few good European officers, his soldiers, drilled and disciplined like white troops, would be as a lance with a steel point. The supply was not plentiful; but it was not wholly wanting. Younger sons of French families were more ready to wander than they have been since the Revolution; and, sooner or later, a few British, or Indo-British, officers became available. These men cut loopholes in the jungle with their swords, admitting a little air and light.

But the general effect, down to the time when the servants of the Company appeared in Hindustan, is that of hardly-mitigated anarchy; and much the same would even now arise if anything should occur to cause the disappearance of the employees of the British Government.

The story to be told involves details bearing on the insecurity of order, property and life, the absence of police, the great prevalence of all sorts of crime, the inability of the different persons who professed themselves rulers to collect revenue by ordinary methods, or with any attempt at regularity. Hence the agriculturists, besides the general uncertainty of their lives, had to suffer from this further annoyance, that their affairs wavered between times when no revenue was demanded from them, so that they could waste their profits upon fakirs and fireworks, and other times when the Government sent troops to the villages who took everything on which they could lay hands.

The famous Moghal Empire of Hindustan had been founded in the sixteenth century of our era by the Timuride Babar, and lasted, in more or less vigour, for seven generations. In 1724 the Prime Minister, Chin Kulich Khan, deserted the sinking ship and established an independent power at Haidarabad in the Deccan, where his descendant, with the title of "Nizam," still maintains a semi-monarchical position, though virtually a feudatory of the British Empire.

In 1738 the Persians under Nadir Shah sacked Dehli, the metropolis of Hindustan, making a massacre of the inhabitants, and carrying away untold booty. In three months' time a blow had been struck from which the Empire never rallied. Slowly the welfare of Hindustan ebbed—a spectacle of tardy dissolution. In 1748 the Emperor, in whose reign the sack of Dehli happened, was taken with an attack of the heart as he sat on his ruined throne, of which the jewels and decorations had been stripped off and taken to Persia; and as a contemporary said, "after his demise everything went to wreck, and he may be considered the seal of the House of Timur." A series of puppet kings succeeded, phantoms of empire put up by unscrupulous politicians one day, to be removed the next, until the murder of the Emperor Alamgir II., in 1757—while the heir-apparent was pursuing a course of adventure in Bengal—left the throne without an occupant. A literal Anarchy.

It was on such a scene that the British entered, led by Robert Clive, fresh from triumph over the French in South India. Four competitors were now appearing to contest the Empire of India with Shah Alam, the wandering heir: two were European—the English and the French; two Asiatic—the Marathas and the usurping Muslim of Mysore. Of these the French had lost, or all but lost, their chance. The power of the English Company had struck a tap-root into the soil of the Carnatic, and was now spreading its branches over Bengal. The Marathas had just experienced a sharp reverse in Upper India, whence the Afghans had driven them with frightful carnage, as will be found related in the monograph on Sindhia, the first in the "Rulers of India" series. In Mysore the adventurer Haidar Ali had set aside the native dynasty, and was founding the short-lived but formidable State which was destined to be overthrown by Lord Wellesley at the end of the century. Meantime Haidar was not only keeping the Marathas at bay, but was threatening his Mohammedan brethren at Haidarabad. Such was the political state of India when the Great Anarchy began.

CONTENTS

LIST OF ILLUSTRATIONS

CHAPTER I

Difference between progressive races and unprogressive races—The steel head needed for the bamboo lance—The Greeks in India—The Portuguese at Goa—The French in the Carnatic—Mahadaji Sindhia on white troops.

OF all historic world-dramas none has been more enduring than that which presents the secular conflict of Europe and Asia; the tribes of movement and the tribes of repose; the national forces that are static and the national energies that are dynamic. Beginning with the crime and punishment symbolised in the story of Cain, we find kindred races always acting under opposite impulses; and even when (as under the Achæmenids) Asia was the aggressor, Europe always conquered in the long run. This was noticed by Hippokrates, who accounted for it by observing that, while the Greeks fought for their country, the Persians fought only for their king.

The difference is the more remarkable by reason of the antagonism to which it has given rise. The energetic son of the frost, constrained to extort from Nature the niggard elements of existence, has been always contemptuous, while the vexation of the more restful native of sunnier lands has too often become hatred for those by whom his quiet has been disturbed: the Sepoy Mutiny of 1857, and the attack on the Pekin Legations in 1900, are among the more familiar modern instances of bloody but hopeless effort. In the long run discipline and moral superiority are rewarded by success; although this, indeed, has not been the rule always. Xenophon was a mere leader of mercenaries; Alexander was a marauding despot; Julian and Valerian were unable to prevail. In the Crusades of the Middle Ages fortune still was variable; and Bajazet overthrew the Christians at Nikopolis with frightful slaughter, though the latter had some amount of patriotism for their support. Under Mohammed II. the Byzantine rump of the Roman Empire was entirely extirpated, and his successors gained several temporary successes over the Christian armies. Yet, on the whole, the tide was ebbing: the Moors were expelled from Spain, the Turks were rolled back from Austria; the European armies everywhere surpassed in skill, science, and cohesion, prevailing over the more numerous, but less disciplined hosts of their opponents, until the French in the Carnatic found out a solution in setting the ranks of the one under the leadership of the other. With a small head of sharp steel, the long lance has learned to follow.

That the Oriental warrior is by no means bound to be personally inferior to the European in valour or endurance has been shown in many instances, from the Punjab wars of the middle of the nineteenth century to the Frontier campaigns that have marked its close. But other things must be equal before the two can meet on equal terms; so long as the civilised Power has abundant supplies of civilised officers it will ultimately prevail, even though its foes be ever so numerous, and even though its men be of the same race, wholly or in large part, as those against whom they are to fight. The barbarian, left to the control of his own chiefs, loses confidence and resolution, so that ten men may chase a thousand. In the battle of Plassy (1757) Clive repulsed a regular army, 50,000 strong, horse and foot, with 40 guns, having less than 3,000 men with him, of whom only 800 were white troops; he had no cavalry and only 8 guns. At Dehli, in 1857, a force of 50,000 disciplined troops, with a vast artillery, a first-class arsenal and fortifications constructed by our own engineers, were held at bay by a mixed army of natives and British, of whom there were never 5,000 fit for duty, but who finally stormed their defences and broke their array for good and all.

The apparent exception in the South African War at the end of the nineteenth century and the beginning of the twentieth is not real. The British troops had the superiority in other respects besides numbers; but the enemy had officers acquainted with the country, and began the quarrel with vast resources in money and the materials of war. And they were not Orientals, but a resolute yeomanry of considerable fighting power. The rule that Oriental multitudes cannot contend against the white man is one that may be taken to be universal.

The complete explanation of this persistent fact may be a matter for discussion; of its existence there can be no doubt. Whether due to climate, or to institutions, the ultimate victory always falls to the men of the West; and amongst immediate causes must be reckoned the inability of Oriental officers to lead. For the most part corrupt and wanting in any cause more noble than their own sordid interests, they fail to inspire in their men that sense of trust in themselves and in each other which gives solidarity to a body of men. The soldiers may be as brave and devoted as the Turkish privates—for example—have always been; but that perfection of discipline must always be lacking which is what we speak of as "the steel lancehead"; the officers bid their men to go on when they ought to be showing them the way.

Necessarily the combination of a nucleus of white soldiers will turn the scale in Eastern warfare. This was long ago shown—perhaps for the first time at the battle of Cunaxa (B.C. 401)—where the Greeks held their ground and killed more than their own number of the Persian enemy, even though the death of Cyrus hindered a perfect victory. Though the royal army numbered, it is said, 400,000, the Greeks retired to their camp in good order, and made such terms that their retreat was practically secure. Without guides they made their way through the snows of Armenia and the harassing Kurds; starved and fevered, they at last reached the shores of the Euxine, having lost only 14 per cent. of their number on the long and perilous march.

Three quarters of a century later, Alexander led a Grecian army to the same regions; but his campaigns only exemplify a portion of our argument. The victories over Darius Codomannus, and over Porus, the Punjab King, were won by a man of high military genius at the head of a considerable army of European veterans; and in such cases there could be little doubt as to the result. But the position of Seleukos, and of the Hellenic rulers who succeeded him in Central Asia, affords a stronger instance of the value of Western character. The Macedonians not only held Syria, but dominated Turkestan and the regions on the Parapomisus, for full two hundred years, at one time ruling from the Euphrates to the Indus. Absorbed at last, and hemmed in on all sides, they finally disappeared; but not before they had planted Western arts and institutions in Mesopotamia, Khorasan, and Bactria. Gradually, in what manner is not exactly known, they were pressed over the Hindukush range by tumultuous movements of Parthian and Scythian hordes, until they finally settled in the hills and plains on the Upper Indus. They even reached the lands between that river and its tributary—now known as the Jhelam—on whose banks Alexander had won his great battle. Here, stretching from Kashmir to Multan, was their last great settlement; and here, without means of communication or reinforcement from Europe, they became gradually assimilated to the Scytho-Buddhist system before which they had long been drifting. This occurred about the beginning of the Christian era; but was not accompanied by any violent catastrophe and did not cause any sudden destruction of such residue of civilisation as had been up to that time preserved. We are informed by Plutarch—writing in the first century A.D.—that Alexander had "inspired India with the arts of Hellas"; and Ælian, about one hundred years later, recorded that the Persian and Indian Kings amused their leisure with hearing recitations from the poems of Homer. All these temporary successes of the European intellect, attested, as they are, by the evidence of coinage and sculpture, must have been due to the same mental supremacy of which the episode of the *Anabasis* was a capital, if transient, example in another field.

Faint, therefore, as these traces may seem, they are interesting signs of influence that only needed more favouring conditions to develop into more enduring action. In the remains of Greek culture still forthcoming in that corner of India—especially in the series of coins, at present incomplete—we find unquestionable evidence of skill and character asserted in difficult circumstances, and maintaining for a considerable period some of the distinguishing features of European civilisation amidst environments of a discouraging kind. The Indo-Greek Kings assumed the high title of "Basileus" in courts and camps which were long frequented and admired. So long as communications remained open, they were supplied with imported women of their own race; and when the last of these kings—by name Menander—became a convert to Buddhism, the colony slowly merged in the surrounding population. But they left their mark in the superscriptions of their Scythian successors, whose coinage for some time retained the Greek language, with much of Greek art in the designs. Jupiter passed into Shiva, or Buddha; and Kadphises called himself "Basileus." These obscure but interesting phases of history have been put together and set forth, with equal research and eloquence, by Count Goblet d'Alviella, sometime Rector of Brussels University (*Ce que l'Inde doit à la Grèce*, Paris, 1897).

But it is time to turn to matters of more recent actuality.

For fifteen centuries after the conversion of Menander, European intercourse with India was sparse and transitory. The Romans traded with what are now Gujarat and Sindh; traces of decadent art are still found in those regions, and Latin writers refer to commercial intercourse; but of political or military influences no trace is forthcoming until the bombardment of Calicut by the ships of the Portuguese under Don Vasco da Gama, in 1501 A.D. Nine years later, Albuquerque had a busy year with the Muslim ruler of Bijapur—Yusaf Adil Shah—from whom he finally took Goa in the end of November, 1510; the city was given up to plunder for three days, the Muslim inhabitants being massacred in cold blood.

This conquest, in its ultimate results, gave to the crown of Portugal a capital, religious, commercial and political and a territory of more than one thousand square miles, in which was founded a colony somewhat resembling that of the Greeks in the Punjab, only preserved from the same fate ultimately by the accidental support of other nations. During the first century or so of its existence, the settlement enjoyed great apparent prosperity; during the years of struggle when the British in India were almost hopelessly fighting for existence, "Goa presented a scene of military, ecclesiastical, and commercial magnificence which had no parallel. . . . The brilliant pomp and picturesque display were due to the fact that it was not only a flourishing harbour but also the centre of a great Power. The Portuguese based their dominion in India on conquest by the sword" (*Imperial Gazetteer*, v. 101).

But the foundations of this imposing edifice were defective. Fanaticism and luxury corrupted the colony; every European assumed the airs of an aristocrat, the ladies being shut up in the Oriental manner, while the gentlemen went abroad in silk attire, riding with jewelled trappings and stirrups of gilded silver. "Almost every traveller who visited Goa during its prime tells the same curious story regarding the rashness with which the Portuguese matrons pursued their amours. . . . And the Goanese became a byword, as the type of an idle, a haughty and a corrupt society" (Ibid., p. 102).

Nor was this the worst. Apart from the ruin prepared by the vices of their own conduct, the colonists were beset by the ceaseless hostility of the surrounding natives, excited by the ruthless violence with which they persecuted the local creeds and attempted the propagation of their own faith. The Portuguese, blending the Peninsular attributes of bigotry and a belated chivalry, had neither forgotten the Crusades nor remembered how completely unsuccessful those romantic endeavours had ultimately been. With a tenacity worthy of respect, they blended a deplorable hardness of heart and a fatuous desire to make the natives conform to their beliefs which was no better than ludicrous. Devotion to a high aim was, indeed, not wanting; and the proselytising fervour bore fruit in monuments of sumptuous splendour, some of which are still to be seen erect among the palm groves and jungles of Velha Goa. The better side of this appears in the unselfish labours of St. Francis Xavier—not, however, a Portuguese by birth—by the educational work of the Franciscan Order in Portuguese India, and by the superb churches and colleges built in the chief cities. The darker aspect began to show itself as early as the reign of John III., an able civil ruler, but a fanatic. Under him the Inquisition was established in Portugal and its dependencies; "and it was directly due to his example that the fatal policy of religious persecution was introduced into India" (Morse Stephens, *Albuquerque*, in "Rulers of India").

Two generations later, the Spanish King, Philip II., assumed the government, on the disappearance of Don

Sebastian; and we may be sure that the work of the Inquisition did not suffer at the hands of Alva's master. At the same time the rivalry of northern nations was widening the breach already begun by bigotry and moral deterioration. The Dutch were on the crest of the wave that was rising against Spain in the Netherlands; and it was not to be expected that they would abstain from molesting the dependencies of a kingdom against which they were already urged by the stimulus of commercial competition. While these hardy and not very scrupulous Teutons were blockading Goa and driving the Portuguese from minor settlements on the Malabar Coast and in Ceylon, the English were sapping their maritime power at sea; and the recovery of the Portuguese Crown by a native dynasty found its Indian possessions reduced to the dimensions which they still hold by British sufferance.

It is, however, worthy of note that the fall of Portuguese power in Western India was in no degree due to any military reverses at the hands of the native Powers. Weak as the colony became, it always held its own against Hindu and Mohammedan assaults, however numerously supported and by whatever momentary successes attended. On the other side of India, indeed, the similar efforts of the Native Powers were more permanently successful. Hugli, near Calcutta, was founded by the Portuguese in 1537, but soon became an object of hostility to the Moghal Government. About a century later, the Emperor Shah Jahan, having been offended by various marks of religious and political insolence, gave orders that the Portuguese should be expelled: what followed was almost an anticipation of Cawnpore in the Mutiny.

The year 1631 had been a dry season in Bengal, and an attempt to send away the non-combatant Christians by ship failed by reason of the shallow state of the Hugli river, which caused the boats to take the ground, the main stream then flowing in another channel. Consequently the Moghal commander was enabled to make a complete investment of the town and blockade it by land and water. The garrison was of small number, but the Muslim long feared to deliver an assault. At length, after an interval of three and a half months, the besiegers blew up a part of the defences by mining, and, in the confusion, effected an entrance into the town; the fort then capitulated on promise of life; but over a thousand armed Europeans were slain, and the rest of the population removed as prisoners to Agra.

Before the end of the seventeenth century the degeneracy of the Portuguese was deplored by the French traveller Bernier, who at the same time predicted that a French force under Condé or Turenne would "trample under foot" all the armies of the Moghal Empire. The vaunt was to be verified in the course of the next hundred years: the French were the first to point the bamboo lance with steel. The settlement at Pondichéri was founded in 1674 by François Martin; and when, a quarter of a century later, he was besieged there by the Dutch, a portion of his garrison consisted of natives of India, dressed, disciplined and armed in the European style—in a word, what have been known later as "sepoys."

One of Martin's successors, Dumas, did much to develop this system, and in 1735 handed over to his successor a well-drilled force of native infantry, stiffened by a small nucleus of Europeans. Eleven years later, the French, under Labourdonnais, captured Fort St. George at Madras, the principal military post of the British on the Coromandel Coast, and, before the end of the year, fought a Moghal army which had come to the relief of the British and gave them two beatings, the last being decisive. The Muslim leader had 10,000 troops, a large portion of whom were cavalry; the French commanders, Paradis and Esprésménil, had 430 Europeans and 700 sepoys, besides the assistance of a handful of men from the Fort. This action—known in history as the battle of S. Thomé—is said by an English historian to have "inverted the position of the European settler and the native overlord." It at least demonstrated the permanent superiority of civilised over barbaric warfare.

The first person to take particular notice of the essential superiority of the Occidental as a fighting man was an astute Hindu of this period, Madhava, or Mahadaji, Sindhia, the founder of the present House of Gwalior. In the year 1778 the British authorities of Bombay sent a column towards the Deccan which was met and opposed by a Maratha force under the chief command of Sindhia. On January 9, 1779, the column arrived at Talegaon Dabhara, about twenty miles from the city of Poona, where they were suddenly encompassed with a ring of fire. They fought for two days, and then, throwing their guns into a tank, retreated to Wadgaon, three miles to the rearward. Decimated and disheartened, the force here surrendered; and the British officers were summoned to durbar to treat of the terms of surrender. It is on record that, in that moment of passing triumph, Sindhia said to a British officer who sat by him: "What soldiers you have! Their line is like a brick wall; and when one falls, another steps into the gap: such are the troops I would wish to lead." This remark rests on the two-fold testimony of Sir John Malcolm and Captain Grant Duff, both conversant with the traditions of those days: and Sindhia soon acted upon the opinion so expressed. If he could not have British soldiers, he would at least engage the services of European officers and impart to his troops a tincture of European discipline. The ablest and most successful of the military adventurers of the eighteenth century in India was an officer twice chosen by Mahadaji. This was the famous General de Boigne; but before him we must briefly notice a few earlier labourers in the same field.

CHAPTER II

Monsieur Law, the Franco-Scot—Walter Reinhardt, alias General Sombre—Médoc.

THE first, in point of time, among the men we are considering was Monsieur Law—the "Mushir Lass" of native writers—a nephew of the Scotsman, John Law of Lauriston, whose financial schemes did so much mischief to France during the Regency. His career as an adventurer was neither long nor glorious; but he was a professional officer, and began military life with good prospects, distinguishing himself particularly in 1748, when Admiral Boscawen was repulsed in his attempt to besiege Pondichéri. The Governor of the French Settlement at that time was the famous Dupleix, then engaged in his life-struggle with the British, from whom he had taken Madras and seemed in a fair way to wrest their whole power and existence in India. Direct war between the rival nations ought to have ceased in 1749, when the treaty of Aix-la-Chapelle became known in India; but Dupleix, by taking up the cause of two Muslim claimants, was held by the Madras authorities—restored by the treaty—to be aiming at the position of Lord-paramount over Southern India. They, therefore, brought forward two competitors, and thus—under guise of a war of succession—the rival European Powers were opposed again. Dupleix at that time seemed to have the omens in his favour. In the beginning of 1751 both the French candidates were in possession, the one as Viceroy of the Deccan—what is now called "Nizam"—the other, as his Nawab or Deputy, in the Carnatic, or Province of Arcot, in which Madras was situated. The British aspirant for the latter was hemmed in by a superior force at Trichinopoly, and the fall of that place seemed imminent, when the genius of a "heaven-born captain" turned the scale. With a handful of men and a few small guns, Clive dashed upon Arcot in the month of August; and, the hostile garrison hurrying out on the other side, the town was held for the claimant favoured by the British. Dupleix saw the necessity of a counter-blow; but being at the moment left without a general, resolved, in an evil hour, to give the command to Law, who had been home to France since the siege of Pondichéri, and had just returned to duty in high health and spirits.

As this is not the history of the war, it may be enough to sum up the story of the investment of Trichinopoly in a few words. Law proved his unfitness for command in every instance: the British leaders, Lawrence, Clive, and Dalton, were men of energy and resource; and Law's part in the war ended, in the middle of June, 1752, with the surrender to them of himself and 35 officers, with nearly three thousand men. A brilliant summary of these operations is to be found in Macaulay's Essay on Clive. For fuller details Malleson's *History of the French in India* will be found both interesting and impartial.

What efforts were possible Dupleix continued to make, until his recall some two years later; but everything was against him, and he was at last sacrificed to the unjust impatience of an ungrateful nation. Meanwhile Law, finding all prospects clouded in the South, had gone to Bengal, on being set at liberty after the Convention of Sadras in 1754.

Two years later, when Sirāj-ud-daulah made that attack on Calcutta which led to the Black Hole and all its consequences, Law was Agent to the French Company at

Kasimbazar, near the capital of the Moghal Nawab, or Deputy, of Bengal, the temporary victor. When, in the following year, Law's ancient antagonist, Clive, came up to retrieve the British position in Bengal, one of his earlier measures was the siege of Chandernagar, the French headquarters. Bombarded from the river, the place capitulated; but a few of the French officers, with about fifty white soldiers and twenty sepoys, marched out and joined Law. Kasimbazar was accordingly threatened by the conquerors, who disregarded the fact that the French there enjoyed the nominal protection of the Nawab. That unhappy chief, seeing no immediate object in breaking with the British, dismissed Law and his men, furnishing them with supplies and undertaking to recall them if, as was expected, war should soon break out. "Recall us?" Law answered, prompted by experience of Clive and his own British blood. "Alas! Your Highness will never see us again."

Law's prophecy was fulfilled: in June the Nawab, betrayed by his most trusted officer, was defeated at Plassy and soon afterwards captured and put to death by the traitor's son. Law and his associates wandered up the country and offered their swords to the Hindu Raja Ramnarain, who was in charge of the Province of Bihăr. Pursued by Colonel (afterwards Sir) Eyre Coote, they took refuge in the territory of the Nawab of Oudh, finally engaging in the service of the Crown Prince, who had fled from Dehli and was bent upon obtaining reinforcement in that quarter.

This period—that immediately succeeding the battle of Plassy—deserves attention on more grounds than one. It was then that men's minds began to be occupied with what is now the Lieutenancy of Bengal; the Company at home beginning to see that the efforts of their servants in the South-east—however successful over the French—were somewhat of a false start, so far as access to the heart of the Indian Empire was concerned; while the French officers who had lost their occupation in the Deccan were at the same time throwing an anxious eye towards the future. "So far as I can see," said Law to the native historian of the time, "there is nothing that you could call 'Government' between Patna and Dehli. If men in the position of Shuja-ud-daulah (the Nawab of Oudh) would take me up loyally, I would not only beat off the English, but would undertake to administer the Empire."[1]

Associated with Law in this arduous enterprise were men, some of whose names will recur on the following pages; Médoc, Reinhardt, Du Drenec, and others of whom no definite record remains, such as the Comte de Moidavre, and the Chevalier de Crecy; M.M. St. Frais and Courtin, who had served hopelessly but bravely at Plassy, were captured by Coote on their way to Lucknow in 1758.

We have now to follow the fortunes of the remaining fugitives, so far as fact or fancy will lead us. Without authoritative commissions or regular pay, far from letters, books or any of the resources of civilisation, they wandered over the alluvial plains, steaming with monsoon miasma, or basking in deadly heat, sometimes feasted by Nawabs, at other times living on the scanty fare of the bazars; everywhere followed by the relentless British, yet keenly cherishing the hope of revenge and altered fortune. At last they found a momentary refuge with the Crown Prince—as forlorn as themselves—in Bundelkhand, where a Hindu chief had lately founded a small principality named, after himself, Chhatarpur.

Early in 1760, however, came news from Dehli which led the Prince to fresh enterprise; his father, the Emperor, had been murdered by a ruthless minister, and the Prince also learned that the Afghans had invaded the Punjab and occupied Dehli. Apparently afraid to return, he assumed the succession, with the title of Shah Alam, at a

[1] *Siar-ul-mutakharin*, by Ghulām Hossain Khan.

village in Bihār called Kanauti, and called on all loyal servants of the Crown to give him aid where he was.

"The Eastern Subahs"—to use a phrase of the old historians—were, at the time of the Prince's proclamation held by a nominee of the British to whom Clive had been partly indebted for his rapid triumph. This nobleman was Jāfar Ali Khan, the "Meer Jaffier" of history, and his deputy in Bihār was the Raja Ramnarain, who was mentioned above as holding the same post under the older government. This latter, having sent to Jāfar for help, came forth from the sheltering walls of Patna to oppose the proceedings of his sovereign, the titular Emperor, Shah Alam; but the Imperialists repelled him with serious loss, in which was included that of four companies of British sepoys with their officers. On this the Raja, wounded and alarmed, fell back on Patna, which, for the moment, was not besieged.

Shortly after this success, the Emperor encountered an Anglo-Bengali force; and, not prevailing, adopted—probably on Law's advice—the soldierly expedient of a flank-march, hoping to cut between the enemy and his capital of Murshidabad and seize upon that city in the absence of its defenders. But he was once more baffled by the superior activity of the British leaders, and in April turned to the only course left him, the siege of Patna. The batteries were quickly established, and Law effected a breach, after five days of open trenches, proceeding at once to the assault before the Anglo-Bengali troops should have time to come up and raise the siege. The stormers reached the ramparts with help from scaling ladders, the breach so hurriedly attempted being far from complete. On reaching the top, the Imperialists were met by the flower of the garrison, animated by the presence of Dr. Fullarton, a British Medical Officer; and the assailants drew off for a time. The attack, however, was twice renewed, and the defenders of Patna were on the point of being overpowered when help appeared from an unexpected quarter. Captain Knox, sent from Murshidabad to watch the Imperialists, had run across the interposed three hundred miles in thirteen days. Falling upon the Emperor's army at the hour—1 p.m.—when the men were resting after dinner, without accoutrements or arms, he put them to flight with his small following, of whom only two hundred were Europeans.

After some manœuvring and another unsuccessful flight the Imperialists took up their winter quarters between Patna and Murshidabad, near the town of Gya. But Law's course was now all but run. On January 15, 1761, the British, who had become of sufficient strength to assume the offensive, attacked the Imperial forces at Suăn, and the result was the flight of the Emperor and his native followers. In the deserted field the British commanders, Major Carnac and Captain Knox, came upon a small group consisting of about fifty foot and thirteen French officers, in the midst of whom was Law, seated astride on a now idle field-piece, with the colours of his command in his hand. Wearied with his long and fruitless wanderings, he invited death; but the British officers, approaching with uncovered heads, besought him to surrender. "To that," said the Franco-Scot, "I have no objection if you leave me my sword, which I will not part with as long as I am alive." The Major consenting, the late adversaries shook hands, and Law was taken to camp in Carnac's palanquin, which was at hand. This is our last authentic view of a brave, but very unlucky man; and we are indebted for it to Ghulăm Hossain, who was much impressed by the humanity and courtesy of the scene.

One of the most remarkable among Law's followers was Walter Reinhardt, believed to have been born in the small electoral Province of Trèves, about 1720. The ties of country were not strong at that time in border-lands like that, and young Reinhardt, enlisting in the French army, found himself, in the course of the service, stationed at Pondichéri at the time when Labourdonnais and Dupleix were making their most vigorous efforts to obstruct the designs of the British Company. After the operations already glanced at, Reinhardt was included in the surrender of Law's force at Trichinopoly in 1752, upon which he took service in a British regiment. In 1756 he deserted and again joined the French, accompanying Law to Bengal in the capacity of sergeant.

In 1760 occurred the palace revolution by which the Nawab Jāfar was deposed and Kāsim Ali — "Meer Cossim"—set up in his place. Not being disposed to accept the part of a regal mute, this new ruler set about providing himself with a regular army, to the command of which he appointed an Armenian, called by the native historians Gurjin Khan, under whom Reinhardt obtained command of a battalion of foot. Stirring events were coming: the Calcutta Council in no long time quarrelled with their nominated Nawab; Mr. Ellis, the local Agent of the Council, attempting to seize Patna, was worsted and shut up there, with one hundred and fifty of his white and coloured followers. Kāsim Ali lost his head and ordered a general massacre. Gurjin and his officers demurred. "Arm the English," they said, "and we will fight them like soldiers. Butchers we are not and will not be." In this emergency recourse was had to Reinhardt, who appears to have undertaken the task without hesitation. The courtyard in which the prisoners were collected was surrounded by Reinhardt's men, who shot them down from the upper terraces; Dr. Fullarton alone was spared.

As some attempt has been made in later days to throw doubt on this account, it may be well to notice some of the evidence on which it rests. Fullarton is not known to have left any written record of the massacre; but his oral account must have been the original authority. Broome, in his admirable *History of the Bengal Army*, accepts it without question; as also does Major L. T.

Smith, of Sindhia's service, who knew the men of that day and their traditions, serving only a quarter of a century after Reinhardt's death. Smith's words are: "He undertook the criminal commission with ardour and alacrity; but I have been credibly informed that this nefarious act haunted his mind to the last hour of his existence." The *Imperial Gazetteer* (xi. 96) accepts the story on the authority of "a contemporary letter." Lastly, it is not easy to see how such a myth could have found currency had it not had some foundation in the known character of the man.

This massacre took place after Kāsim's army had undergone several defeats, in one at least of which Reinhardt—known by the sobriquet of "Sombre"—took a handsome part. The battle of Ghiria, August 3, 1763, was most obstinate, and in the opinion of our officers, the Moghals never fought so well. At one moment they had broken the British line and captured two guns. But discipline prevailed: Kāsim and his swordsmen were put to flight before the end of the year, and forced to seek refuge with Shuja, already mentioned as the Nawab of Oudh. The British demanded their surrender, but Shuja refused; under a curious prejudice of Oriental chivalry he undertook to murder them, if that would do. The battle of Buxar ensued, and the fugitives were driven from the camp of the Nawab, who proceeded to make peace with the victorious British. Sombre—"Somra Sahib," as he had begun to be known among the natives—went to seek his fortune in the disturbed districts south of the Jumna, finally taking service among the Bhurtpur Jats. His following by this time comprised some low Europeans whom he had attracted from among the tramps of the time, with some guns and a few companies of men from the *débris* of Kāsim's army. The total strength was then estimated at four battalions of foot, six field-pieces, chiefly manned by Europeans, and a small corps of native cavalry. Those who are acquainted with the modern

Indian "loafer" can best imagine the sort of ruffians that formed the gunners and officers of this force. Under fire a sort of stolid discipline prevailed; in camp, drunkenness and disobedience ruled supreme. The tactics of the brigade were simple: paying no attention to the general dispositions of the force with which they might be serving, they would enter the field from whatever quarter they deemed suitable; fire their guns with all possible precision as long as their side held its ground; if that side gave way, they would retire their guns under a screen of infantry fire, and, in case of a total defeat, pass over bodily into the service of the victors.

In the autumn of 1774, Sombre Reinhardt was at length enabled to turn these inglorious principles of warfare to a profitable and lasting account. The Emperor had been restored and was now settled at Dehli, whence he despatched his able and high-minded minister—a Persian nobleman named Mirza Najaf Khan—to coerce the Jats who had taken possession of the Imperial city and palace of Agra. Dislodged from this position, they eluded the Imperialists and proceeded to threaten Dehli, accompanied by Sombre and his brigade, halting at Sikandrabad, thirty-six miles from the capital, for the rainy season. On the approach of the cold weather the Mirza marched against them, with 10,000 men, under his godson, Najaf Kuli—a converted Hindu—the "Red battalion" of the Emperor's guards and a choice body of Persian horse forming the rest of his army. After some manœuvres and minor collisions, the Mirza brought the Jats to a stand at Barsāna, in what is now the District of Mathra. Sending on skirmishers from his infantry under Najaf Kuli, and holding his cavalry well in hand, the Imperialist leader began a duel of artillery, in which he lost several Moghal officers and was himself wounded in the arm. Nevertheless his foot and artillery maintained a stout defence while he retired into shelter and had his arm bandaged. Hastening back to the field, he rallied his horsemen with a fervent invocation to the God of battle, and delivered a headlong charge at the centre of the hostile line. His infantry following at the double, the Jats broke and fled, while Sombre's brigade slowly retired in good order and came over the next day. The reinforcement was welcomed; the brigade was taken into the Imperial service, a considerable fief near Dehli being assigned for its support; and its commander was appointed to the charge of Agra, where he passed the residue of his life, taking no further part in active military service.

It is somewhat shocking to our modern notions of historical justice to have to relate this peaceful and honourable conclusion to the career of such a blood-stained and faithless *condottiere*. General Sombre, as he was now called, had a Muslim wife, who went mad; but he had no further trouble to the day of his death, which happened in May, 1778. He was buried in a fine tomb in the Catholic cemetery of the Civil Lines at Agra; and a still more substantial monument remains, in the shape of a church—since converted into a printing-office connected with the convent—where a tablet is still to be seen bearing a Latin inscription. This sets forth that the building was provided at the expense of "Dominus Walter Reinhard," the final *t* being omitted, evidently for the sake of euphony. What became of the fief will be noted later on.

The battle of Barsāna deserves the detailed account above recorded, not only for its illustration of the military habits of Sombre, but still more as an instance of the value of European discipline. Whatever may have been the gallantry of the Mirza and his godson, there can be little doubt that the firmness and energy of the infantry attack by which the charge of cavalry was followed up was mainly due to the discipline of the Mirza's French officers and the initiative which they imparted to their men. Moidavre, Crecy, and Du Drenec were gentlemen of character and experience, much more than a match for the bucolic Jats and Sombre's loafers. But the best known of these officers was Médoc, of whom a brief account must now be given. This adventurer had entered the Jat service about the same time as Reinhardt, though not amongst his followers, having a distinct brigade of his own. A native of Brittany, he had originally come to India with the unfortunate Count Lally, after whose defeats and captivity he had, like many others, found his way to Bengal, where his courage and force of character had attracted a following which grew to a force of five battalions of foot, with twenty guns, and five hundred horse. Shortly after the Restoration, in 1771, he went to Dehli, where he entered the Imperial service and distinguished himself in operations against the Marathas under the orders of Mirza Najaf, as well as in the campaign against the Jats. About 1781 he was despatched to the assistance of the Rana of Gohad, then engaged in a struggle for the fort and district of Gwalior. Here he was surprised, one wet night, by a party of Rohila horse—presumably in the Maratha interest—and forced to retreat upon the old Imperial palace of Fatehpur Sikri, whence he finally made his way to Agra. Here he recruited his men and cast new guns, but is not known to have been actively engaged in the field; and in 1782 he made over his brigade—no doubt for a handsome consideration—to the Rana of Gohad, and returned to France, where he was ultimately killed in a duel.[1] Independently of the battle of Barsāna, Médoc is not distinguished by any military achievement; and his career is remarkable only as showing what might be done for himself, in those wild times, by a soldier of no special intellect. He seems to have founded a family in

[1] Médoc's brigade was not more fortunate after the commander's retreat, having been again surprised by the Marathas, evincing to the last the negligence of a force organised by an officer more remarkable for courage than for conduct.

Brittany, a member of which has been met with in the Channel Islands, in a good social position, within recent times.

A very different man first came to the front during this Gwalior War ; but the military career of Count de Boigne demands a separate chapter.

CHAPTER III

General Martin—Early life of Benoît Boigne—His Indian commencements and engagement by Sindhia—Temporary retirement.

HITHERTO we have been considering cases, for the most part, of men driven from employ by the ill-success of French enterprise in the Carnatic. Another of these was Claude Martin, whose name has been preserved from oblivion by the noble foundations that still bear his name in Lucknow, Calcutta, and Lyons, his native city. Martin never had an opportunity of achieving warlike honours after leaving the French service, which he did about 1762. It is true that he entered the army of the victorious English Company, in which he was allowed to rank until he ultimately reached the titular position of Major-General. But his life was henceforth passed at Lucknow, whither he had been sent on special duty, and where he devoted himself to the arts and crafts, making guns and small-arms for the Nawab, and embarking in successful speculations connected with indigo and other local produce. This quiet career hardly entitles Martin to a place in our list of Military Adventurers; yet so useful a life deserves a passing tribute. He continued his labours for a third of a century, and died in 1800, leaving the bulk of his property to purposes of education in the various places above named. His life was thus described by a contemporaneous observer in 1789:—

"Colonel Martin is a man desirous of all kinds of knowledge; and, although he is at the head of a large property which he owes only to his own industry, he works whole days together at all the arts that concern watchmaking and gunsmith's work with as much bodily labour as if he had his bread to earn by it. As an architect—and he is everything—he has built himself at Lucknow a strong, elegant house." It is said that the Nawab was so delighted with this building, which was known as "Constantia," that he offered to buy it for a sum equivalent to a million sterling. But the General—who had other ends in view—declined the offer, of which the only result was to suggest a singular expedient to prevent the appropriation of the property after his death. A Muslim ruler might violate the rights of a deceased owner, but he would probably respect a tomb. With keen perception of this feature of Oriental character, the General bequeathed the building to the school he intended to found—still known as "La Martinière"—ordering, at the same time, that his body should be interred in one of the ground-floor apartments; and there his remains are still believed to lie, in a plain sarcophagus of marble, though disturbed by rebels in 1857.

This is a singular instance of a victory of peace which is pleasant to contemplate among the more turbulent scenes with which our story is chiefly occupied.

A friend and partner of Martin's, who also did good with a great fortune, now demands attention. In the brief notice of Médoc we have had to refer to the little war between Sindhia and the Rana of Gohad; this was originally waged for the possession of Gwalior; but that place was captured by a British expedition, under Major Popham, in 1780, handed over to the Rana of Gohad, and left to be recaptured by Sindhia, in pursuance of the negotiations which began in the following year, and ended in the Treaty of Salbai in 1782. Not content with this, the Maratha chief next aspired to deprive the Rana of Gohad itself; and while engaged in this attempt, discovered, among the stolen property of a European traveller, a detailed plan of much ability intended to be submitted to the Rana for the purpose of enabling him to raise the siege. He found that the traveller was named Benoît Boigne, who was seeking for employment among his—Sindhia's—enemies; and, having a sort of tacit understanding with Warren Hastings, the British Governor-General, with whose passport the foreigner was travelling, he wrote to Hastings and procured M. Boigne's recall. The circumstances which led to these events—destined as they were to have most important consequences—deserve a brief record.

Benoît Boigne was the son of a respectable burgess of Chambéry in Savoy, born in, or about, 1750, and destined for the profession of arms. While still very young he entered the French service, being posted as an Ensign to the regiment of Lord Clare, in the Irish Brigade, then under the command of Colonel Leigh. It was, doubtless, in that period of his life that he laid the foundation of his knowledge of the English language. France at that time had no work for her soldiers, and after a few years of garrison life the young Savoyard accompanied his corps to Mauritius, returning to France in 1773. Impatient of the want of action and promotion in the then existing state of the service, he took furlough; and, providing himself with a letter of introduction from the Marquis d'Aigueblanche, repaired to the camp of the Russian Admiral Orloff, then heading the forces of Catherine II. in a war against the Ottoman Empire. Appointed Captain in a regiment of Greeks, he was captured by the Turks during the siege of Tenedos, and kept in confinement at Scio until the peace of Kuchuk Kainarji, in June, 1774.

Obtaining his liberation under this treaty, Boigne repaired to St. Petersburg, where he was presented to the Empress, and made upon that able but sentimental sovereign the impression natural to a skilful soldier who was also a fine young man. Catherine engaged Captain

Boigne to take a journey in her interest to the East, and on his way through Southern Russia he had the fortune to fall in with the eldest son of the Duke of Northumberland, who gave him some letters of introduction. Proceeding to Aleppo, the young officer joined the Bassora caravan, with which he hoped to visit Persia; but, after reaching Baghdad, the party were stopped by the Persian officials, that kingdom being then at war with Turkey. Nothing daunted, Boigne retraced his steps and proceeded to Alexandria; and, after some further adventures in Egypt, decided on visiting India, took ship at Suez, and in due course landed at Madras. Here Lord Percy's letters befriended him, and in the beginning of 1778 he was appointed to a vacant commission in the 6th regiment of Native Infantry, having thus held a commission in the service of three several nations before he was thirty years old.

The Government of Fort St. George (Madras) was at this period in sore straits, neither civil chiefs nor military possessing the capacity needed to bring their afflictions to a happy issue; the Governor was Mr. Whitehill, who had to be removed from office by Warren Hastings; the Commander of the Forces was Sir Hector Munro, who had won the battle of Buxar fifteen years before, but to whom years had brought more of discretion than of valour. Haidar Ali, the Muslim usurper of Mysor, had nursed his grievances against the Presidency until he could contain them no more, and his son, Tippu Sahib, exceeded him in malignity, if not in military genius. Two Members of Council went in succession to ask for peace, each in turn to be driven with contumely from the enemy's camp; the disinterested pleadings of the missionary Swartz were no more successful. In June, 1780, the Mysoreans burst like a flood into the Carnatic lowlands with 90,000 troops of all arms and a number of French officers. Of all the wars of modern times in India none has had more sympathy from the popular side; public prayers were everywhere offered for the success of Haidar and his son; the commissariat was ably administered by a wealthy Brahman. The Madras rulers could oppose to the invaders only a force of about 5,200 men assembled at the Mount under Munro, and a smaller body under Colonel Baillie, in the "Northern Circars," which they ordered down to join the Commander-in-Chief, who was marching towards Conjeveram. It is well known that, after delays for which he was not perhaps entirely answerable, the latter did not arrive at his destination till near the end of August, while Baillie never reached it at all, being cut up by Tippu without any attempt at relief from headquarters' camp, where the firing had been audible for hours. The lives of the surviving British officers were spared on the strong representations of the Frenchmen present, but they were destined to a long and painful captivity. The regiment to which our Savoyard adventurer belonged was involved in this catastrophe, and subsequent history would have been seriously affected had he not been previously detached on escort duty with two companies, and so escaped the fate of his comrades.

But he had seen enough of Madras imbecility, and soon after resigned his commission, setting up at the Presidency as a fencing-master. After a few months of this unpromising life, our adventurer appears to have remembered his commission from the Czarina, or his own wish to explore the then mysterious regions of Central Asia. A new Governor had come out to Madras in the shape of Lord Macartney, who had also seen Russia and known what it was to be a prisoner of war. To this nobleman our adventurer addressed himself for aid, and not in vain. Struck, perhaps, by sympathetic feelings, he dismissed Boigne with a letter for Warren Hastings, armed with which the Savoyard reached Calcutta in the beginning of 1783.

His military career now seemed closed: whatever

technical knowledge he may have acquired, it had brought him neither glory nor experience of war on a serious scale; and not even the sagacious ruler to whom he now presented himself could have seen that he had before him a man destined to be a great soldier in the same sense as Marshal de Saxe, or Frederic, called "the Great."

Mr. Hastings, understanding that the man before him was undertaking the arduous task of travelling to Russia by way of Persia and Turkistan, readily gave what help lay in his power, supplying letters which might be useful credentials, as he had already done for Bogle when visiting Thibet. Thus provided, the traveller made his way up the country, his first halt being at Lucknow. Here he found affairs in a very different condition from what had been the case when Kāsim and Sombre went there eighteen or nineteen years before. The bold Nawab-Vazir of those days had passed away, and his place had not been filled up; his son, Asaf-ud-daulah, bore, indeed, the same titles, but was in effect little more than a stipendiary, or mediatised prince, secured by British support and spending on frivolous amusement the money extorted from defenceless subjects. Martin was there, leading the life of busy curiosity described in a quotation given above; and Major Middleton, the Governor-General's Agent, doing honour to his employer's credentials, paid the traveller all due attention. Presented to the Nawab, he was favoured with a dress of honour and a gift of 4,000 rupees, and at Lucknow he passed the hot season, studying Persian and making friends.

Meanwhile the Western horizon was clouding over, and the Moghal Empire was relapsing into the decrepitude from which the integrity and courage of Mirza Najaf had given a momentary relief. That able public servant had died in April, 1782, leaving his estate and his office to be objects of contention between Mirza Shafi, his nephew, and a favourite follower called Afrasyāb Khan. The Empire rapidly became disintegrated and anarchy was setting in with its worst train of consequences.

"So reduced," says an eye-witness of those times, "was the actual number of human beings, and so utterly cowed their spirit, that the few villages that continued to exist at great intervals had scarcely any communication with one another; and so great was the increase of beasts of prey that what little communication remained was often cut off by a single tiger known to haunt the road." [1]

Yet the sovereignty of this afflicted region long continued to be a matter of veneration and its service to be sought with eager competition. To understand all the crimes and intrigues that went on over the heads of the unhappy people of Upper India would require reference to a whole literature; we must here be content with what relates to the subject with which our narrative is immediately concerned. Outside the Moghal struggle a wary Maratha was keenly watching; and while the palace and person of the imbecile Emperor were being contested by the courtiers, Sindhia was biding his time. Towards the end of 1783, Mirza Shafi came back from a small foray, bringing with him a Persian leader of mercenaries named Mohammed Beg Hamadāni, to whom was entrusted the governorship of Agra. The Savoyard adventurer also came up at the same time from Lucknow with an introduction to the Mirza, but was prevented from using it by the death of his intended patron, who was just then pistolled by his associate, Mohammed Beg. Boigne next turned to the British Agent in Sindhia's camp, Mr. Anderson, whom he found in attendance on the Maratha chief before the walls of Gohad. From him also he failed to obtain assistance. Being on terms of acquaintance with a Scot, named Sangster, who was in charge of the gun foundry of the besieged Rana, he next

[1] *Memoirs of Jas. Skinner*, by Baillie Fraser.

opened a correspondence with this person, in the hope of being engaged by the Rana; and this led to his being summoned to Calcutta by Warren Hastings, as already stated.

The situation was grave. Boigne must have been aware that, while on the one hand the British authorities were anxious to prop up the decadent Empire, they were on the other hand most reluctant to break with Sindhia, whom Hastings had for some time regarded as the coming man. For his own part, as an independent traveller, he had a perfect right to disregard the mandate of the British ruler; and yet, at the same time, considerations of prudence and of gratitude alike forbade any action on his part which might add to the embarrassments of the Governor-General. Boigne took the wise course of returning to Calcutta, at whatever cost in money and disappointment; and he joined the camp of Mr. Hastings, whom he found marching for the last time to Lucknow, and from whom he once more sought aid.

This prompt obedience was welcome to the much-vexed Governor-General who was winding up his complicated and troublesome affairs preparatory to leaving India for good, and was willing to befriend a man who could be so amenable. Taking Boigne as far as Lucknow, he once more dismissed him with credentials; and the traveller proceeded to Jaipur, where he was well received by the Maharaja, who, nevertheless, to his own great detriment, declined his offer of service. By that time a British Mission had at last appeared at Dehli under Major Browne, and to him Boigne had recourse, on the recommendation of the departing Governor-General. Browne presented the wanderer to the Emperor; but the latter, in his forlorn condition, would take no initiative, and contented himself with a recommendation to Sindhia, by this time completely successful at Gohad, and cantoned at Mathra with an eye to further operations.

What was the attraction between these two able and ambitious men we can only guess. Sindhia, as we have already seen, had a warm appreciation of European warfare, and Boigne would probably discover this and adapt his persuasions to the foregone conclusion. By a strange coincidence he now obtained—after all the toils and disappointments of his past years—the opening that he had so long been seeking from the very chief whose rising star he had once refused to recognise. He was engaged by Sindhia to organise a force of two battalions of infantry, with a salary of Rs. 1,000 *per mensem* for himself and pay for 1,700 men and officers at an average rate of Rs. 8 a head, to be appointed at his discretion. It was but a humble beginning, but it was all that he could obtain—or, perhaps, expect—to start with.

Afrasyāb, the last Moghal obstacle to the ambitious projects of Sindhia, was removed by assassination in October, 1784, in camp before Agra, where Mohammed Beg was holding out for terms. All the chiefs present at once repaired to the tent of Sindhia and unanimously voted him to supreme power at an informal durbar. He then repaired to Dehli, leaving the recalcitrant Beg in temporary occupation of the Agra fort. On arriving at Court, he obtained a patent as Prime Minister, with a grant of the Provinces of Dehli and Agra for the support of his army, contingent only on his making a monthly provision for the Emperor's personal expenses and privy purse.

Meanwhile Boigne had accompanied a body of troops detached for the pacification of Bundelkhand, whence he returned in the spring of 1785. On the 27th of March the fort of Agra was surrendered by Mohammed Beg, who was pardoned and taken into the Imperial service; the palace of Dehli was guarded by a choice body of infantry, and Sindhia retired to his favourite cantonment of Mathra, where he remained until the following spring.

There proved, however, to be much left for Sindhia to do before he could finally establish his position, and M. Boigne, in particular, found himself in difficulties that might have daunted many a hopeful spirit and did actually produce even in him a state of despondency which almost wrecked his career. The Muslim nobles were by no means reconciled to the rule of one whom they regarded as a Hindu upstart; and when, in straits for money, Sindhia took measures for overhauling the titles of their holdings, they began to stir under the fear of confiscation. Mohammed Beg took the lead in these discontents, and on the outbreak of active hostility among the chiefs of Rajputāna, went over to them with the bulk of his troops. In a great battle at Lalsaut, about forty miles from Jaipur, the Beg was killed; but his place was taken by his nephew, Ismail Beg, soon to prove one of the boldest leaders of heavy horse then in the country. The new levies were led in this action by their Savoyard Colonel, but they were not of sufficient strength to do more than protect the retreat. Sindhia was now in a perilous way, cut off from his force in Agra—which was promptly invested—and menaced in his rear by an army of 100,000 brave Rājputs, who were, fortunately, too indolent to follow him with due promptitude. Throwing himself into the almost impregnable fortress of the Jats at Bhurtpur, Sindhia wrote to Poona for the help of a Maratha army, and took steps for the augmentation of his regular forces under Colonel Boigne.

Having at last digested their banquet of victory, the Rājputs advanced to renew the attack on Sindhia. Surprising one of his divisions under a Maratha General, Ambaji Inglia, they put it to flight, and compelled Sindhia to seek shelter in the fort of Gwalior, at the same time that Ismail Beg, before Agra, was reinforced by Ghulām Kādar, the chief of Sahāranpur, at the head of the Duāb. Sindhia, having rallied his forces, sent the bulk of them, with the new levies, to raise the siege of

Agra; but they were once more beaten by the Muslim and driven back on Bhurtpur. Reinforced from Poona, he resumed the offensive; and, in a battle fought near Fatehpur Sikri, the new levies resisted the Moghal cavalry to such effect that the siege of Agra was at last raised, and the Marathas entered the fort which had been the bone of this obstinate contention.

But the Savoyard commander was by no means satisfied. Though he afterwards admitted that this time of trial had been the hour of Sindhia's moral greatness, Boigne did not yet fully believe in that chief; and he was further disappointed by the smallness of his force, the subordination of his standing and the limits of the confidence reposed in him generally. Accordingly, he took advantage of the temporary lull, obtained leave *sine die*, and repaired to his friend, Colonel Martin, at Lucknow, with whom he entered into partnership in business pursuits. The Maratha chief and the European soldier had parted with reciprocal expressions of good will; Sindhia returned to his Mathra cantonment, and the quondam Colonel laid down his sword and devoted himself to the manufacture of indigo.

CHAPTER IV

Ghulām Kādar and Ismail Beg—a Palace Tragedy.

AMONG the men who made havoc in Hindustan during the latter half of the eighteenth century should be noticed the two whose names stand at the head of this chapter. Of these, the one was of Persian extraction, whose uncle, Mohammed Beg, had been a leader of mercenaries, killed at the battle of Lalsaut at the end of May, 1787; the other being the son of a restless and unscrupulous Pathan, or Rohila, named Zalita Khan, whom he had lately succeeded in a small chieftainship in the Upper Duāb. It will be convenient in future to know the latter as the Rohila Nawab, and to bear in mind that he was a young man of strong passions, if not disordered intellect; the Beg, on the other hand, being little more than an intrepid soldier, famous in his time as a leader of heavy cavalry.

Towards the end of the rainy season of 1787 the two leaders, having for the time dispersed the Marathas, advanced upon Dehli. Sindhia, being for the moment powerless to oppose them, retired to his own country to await such reinforcements as the Poona Government might send him, and the confederate leaders had a clear field for their operations. Their object appears to have been to drive back the Marathas and restore the power of Islam in the administration of such provinces as still acknowledged the Imperial sway. The Beg covering Agra and Mathra with a containing force, his associate advanced on Dehli, whence he expelled the small Maratha garrison. By the agency of the comptroller of the household, the Rohila chief was introduced into the Emperor's Durbar, where he applied for the office of Amir-ul-Umra, or Premier, taking up his quarters in the apartments of the palace reserved for the holder of that office. But Begum Sombre presently arriving with her brigade under European officers, he retired across the river, and remained for some time quiet in his camp at Shāhdara.

It will be well at this point to take a hasty glance at the scene of the events which followed. The royal residence has suffered since then both from war and from the requirements of British occupations, but enough remains to enable us to trace the main features. The immediate frontage consisted of a large courtyard, at one end of which the monarch sat for the transaction of business. In the rear is a smaller enclosure leading to the Diwani Khas, or Privy Council Chamber, which is walled with beautifully painted stucco, surmounted with a cornice on which is still to be seen in golden letters the famous inscription familiar to readers of *Lalla Rookh:*

> "If there be an Elysium on earth,
> It is this, it is this, it is this."

But the Elysium had already been desecrated; the gorgeous peacock throne with its priceless jewellery had been carried away by the Persians, and the monarch of the dwindled Moghal Empire was reduced to such a substitute as could be provided by a shattered and tattered bedstead, on which he received his privileged visitors.

Into this scene of splendid ruin the Rohila Nawab forced his way; but his further intrusion was arrested by the return of the Begum Sombre, accompanied by a Maratha officer named Ambagi. As these were supported by a respectable force, the Rohila consented to a compromise, by which he obtained the coveted post; and all the troops on both sides were withdrawn, the Shah being left to the protection of a body of horsemen whom he raised for the purpose by the help of funds obtained by the melting of his plate. The Rohila then departed to join the Beg, who was besieging the fort at Agra, which was held by a strong Maratha garrison. At the end of the cold weather, about March, 1788, Sindhia woke from his apparent apathy, having received reinforcements from the Deccan, and came across the Chambal at Dholpur. The Muslim confederates broke up from before Agra, and gave him battle at Chaksana, eleven miles from Bhurtpur, on the 24th of April. General de Boigne was present, but the army was not commanded by him, but by the promoted water-carrier Rána Khán, who had saved the chief's life in the retreat from Panipat in 1761. The Muslim cavalry were handled with spirit; three of the regular battalions deserted the Marathas in the midst of the action; the Jat horse proved worthless.

The day being lost, Rána Khán retired towards Gwalior, and the Rohila Nawab returned to his own country, which was threatened on the northward side by an incursion of the Sikhs. In repelling this he was successful, the incursion having been driven back, though it took more than two generations for the district of Sahăranpur to recover in some measure from the effect of the devastation. The Rohila and the Beg once more joined their forces, and, leaving a containing force before Agra, marched with the remainder of their troops to the capital, which they reached at the beginning of the hot season, the Shah having at the same time returned from a somewhat futile expedition in which he had endeavoured to procure the adhesion of the Rajput Princes.

Sindhia, having received fresh reinforcements from the Deccan, was enabled to raise the siege of Agra; Ismail Beg was driven off after an encounter near the old palace of Fatehpur Sikri. He crossed the Jumna and, being joined by Ghulām Kādar, went off in his company to Dehli. Leaving Lakwa Dada, one of his best Maratha officers, in charge of Agra, Sindhia fell back upon his favourite cantonment of Mathra, sending a small contingent to protect the Emperor at Dehli. The Muslim leaders encamped at Shāhdara. Scarcity prevailed in the camp. At the same time they intrigued with the Shah's officers with such effect that the Moghal portion of the garrison came over to them ; and Himmat, the leader of the Gosains, withdrew his force. Seeing the Emperor thus deserted, the confederates crossed the river, entered Dehli, and took possession of the citadel and the palace. At the beginning of the monsoon, 1788, they separated, the Beg encamping in the old city to the south of the capital, while the Rohila placed his men in the suburb of Dariaoganj, while he himself returned to his old quarters in the palace. Their plan appears to have been to obtain possession of the administration, while their troops protected them from molestation from the Marathas, and to this must be added the peculiar design of the Rohila, who was bent on discovering some hidden treasure which he imagined to have been concealed in the royal precincts.

From the 29th of July to the 10th of August, he occupied himself in digging up the floors, but failed to find the desired booty. He then turned to personal ill-usage of the Shah and his family, the ladies being turned out of the seclusion in which their lives had been spent and driven forth with violence into the unfamiliar dangers of the streets. On the last-mentioned day he caused the fallen Emperor to be brought before him as he sat on the dismantled throne, and when the old man once more declared—what was no matter of doubt—that there was no such treasure in existence, he leapt from the throne, threw his sovereign on the ground, and blinded him with his own dagger, assisted by his Rohila followers.

The unfortunate Shah was then removed to a part of the palace reserved for political prisoners, and a helpless prince was raised to the titular sovereignty, while the intruding Rohila made himself master of the whole place, even sitting on the throne and puffing tobacco smoke into the face of his puppet. But his punishment was approaching. The honest *sabreur* who had hitherto guarded the left rear of the position now abandoned his caitiff comrade, and with the Beg's departure the Marathas from Agra and Mathra began to close in. At length, on the 7th September, after weeks of unlicensed revel, only interrupted by cruelty and by the deaths of many members of the family from starvation, the Rohila moved his men across the Jumna as an escort for his approaching departure. Abandoned by his associate, the Rohila was no longer in a frame of mind to confront Rána Khán and Boigne's trained battalions, and on the 11th October he set fire to the palace and retired to his camp, fording the river on an elephant. The attempted arson failed; Rána Khán and his advance guard arrived in time to extinguish the conflagration and deliver the Shah and the remnant of his unfortunate family. Having imprisoned the puppet-King and the treacherous chamberlain, to whom so much of the Rohila's evil conduct was attributable, Rána Khán marched in pursuit of the Rohila, who had already decamped and taken refuge in the fort of Meerut, which lay directly on the road to his own country. Here he maintained a spirited defence for some nine weeks; courage of the soldier sort was not wanting in his otherwise worthless character. But he must now have perceived that the game was lost, and that his only hope lay in immediate flight to the Sikh country, where his brother had already found refuge. Accordingly, on the shortest night of the year, he secretly departed by one of those postern doors which are usually found in Indian fortresses, mounted on a horse in whose saddlebags were stuffed the crown jewels which he had carried away from Dehli. Falling into a pit in the darkness, he was captured by some villagers and handed over to Rána Khán. By Sindhia's orders he was slain by tortures that lasted several days, and his mangled body was sent to Dehli and laid before his sightless victim. The jewels were found by one of Boigne's officers, who at once left the service and probably took them back to France.

The crimes of the Rohila Nawab were a combination of treason, greed, and cruelty, but their peculiar atrocity shocked the conscience of an age that was not squeamish. When he brutally asked the Shah, whom he had blinded, what he was looking at, the sufferer replied, "Nothing but the word of God between me and thee," for the miscreant had sworn on the Koran to protect and serve his helpless sovereign. In addition to this black treason, the Nawab had also caused the death of many innocent victims, and had finally left the survivors to perish in the flames that he had kindled before his flight. Various reasons were suggested for these atrocities. It was said that when the restless Zalita went into rebellion eleven years earlier he left his family in one of its strongholds from which he himself had fled, and that his son, whose fate we have been describing, had been taken into the royal household when the fort was captured. And the tale went on to say that the boy had suffered mutilation to fit him for the office of a zenana page. For such an injury it was supposed he had ever sought the opportunity of a cruel revenge. Another suggestion was that his understanding was permanently deranged: and in support of this some singular incidents have been recorded. One day he sent for the young people of the royal family and caused them to dance before him; then, reclining on the throne, he pretended to go to sleep, rising presently to rebuke them for their cowardice in not attempting his life when he appeared to lie at their mercy. At another time he sought to palliate his offences by attributing them to supernatural inspiration. As he was advancing from Agra that summer he went to rest during the heat of the day in a garden by the wayside, and had a vision, he said, of an angel, who smote him on the breast, saying: "Arise! go to Dehli and possess thyself of the palace." The Shah, however, looked upon the conduct of the Rohila as a mere outbreak of cruel treachery, and in the poetical lament with which he relieved the darkness of his captivity compared the young Rohila to "a serpent who had stung the bosom where he had been fostered." [1]

The fate of Ismail Beg was more tardy and less terrible than that of his infamous associate. When he returned from Dehli he did so under a temporary truce with Sindhia's General, Rána Khán; but he had not the spirit of a subordinate, and never re-entered the Maratha's service in which he had been engaged up to the time of his uncle's death. For some twenty months more he continued his adventurous career after the fashion of a mediæval *condottiere*, rallying to his standard such Moghal cavaliers as might be wandering about the country in search of employment: and with these he passed into the service of any malcontent prince who might be disposed to refuse payment of tribute to the now dominant Marathas. Without country, cause, or conviction, his standard of duty consisted in fighting bravely for any chief by whom he might be for the moment engaged, and he represented the last successful attempt of the antiquated system of warfare: with flare of trumpet and roll of kettledrum the Beg and his men charged in full armour upon the trained battalions with which it was the policy of Sindhia to fill his army; but the fiery cavaliers had to reel back unsuccessful, while many an empty saddle told of the cool and precise musketry of their opponents. Before long the inevitable

[1] A literal prose translation of this lament will be found in *The Fall of the Moghal Empire*, third edition, London, 1887, pp. 192-3.

end came; foiled in all his attempts, the Beg took refuge in the fort of Kanaund, just then held by the widowed sister of his late associate, Ghulām Kādar. The Rohila lady had been holding out against the Marathas until Perron was sent against her fort with a siege train. Aided by the Beg, she conducted the defence with spirit, till she was killed in an assault. Finding the garrison indisposed to hold out any longer, and trusting to the word of a European, the Beg surrendered on the promise of his life, and was conveyed as a prisoner to Agra. On the highest point of the fort there, an old house was long pointed out as having been built or inhabited by a Jat named Dan Shah; and in this building Ismail passed the remainder of his life, which was, however, not of long duration. Although he does not appear to have been treated with any peculiar harshness, yet the confinement and dulness must have been very oppressive to one long habituated to a stirring life. He was still living in 1794, and was mentioned by Captain Francklin, a writer of those days, as a dangerous man. The exact date of his death is not known, but it took place while he was yet a captive.

The doings of these leaders had not the same influence on the state of the country as those of one or two European contemporaries; they were rather birds of darkness than harbingers of dawn. But they are deserving of notice as illustrating the condition to which the land had been reduced by anarchy; and the people, harassed by war and famine, must have been deprived of all those things which render the life of the poor endurable. The accounts of the state of the country at the time with which we are dealing are derived from various sources. The best known English writers are Dow and Francklin, but their statements are fully endorsed by good native contemporaries. The Eastern horizon was indeed beginning to show signs of the departure of darkness; the British power in Bihār and

Bengal, if it did not bring immediate prosperity, was producing the peace and calm which are prosperity's best foundation. But in the vast region locally known as Hindustan, stretching from Allahabad to Karnal and from the Vindhyas to the southern slopes of the Himalayas, society was completely paralysed, and the occupations of life were almost at a standstill. The drums and tramplings of Moghal and Maratha were by no means the only molestation of the afflicted world. Roads had ceased to exist; towns were deserted; the intercourse between adjoining villages was made difficult by the prowlings of tigers and wild elephants; while the demoralised peasantry, not knowing who would reap their crops, reduced the labours of cultivation to the lowest level necessary for the production of food for their families. Money was buried underground; no fresh supplies of treasure were to be expected; and whenever the periodical rains failed, production ceased, and many thousands of people perished from starvation. This terrible state of things drew to a close with the events of 1788. The only man capable of restoring order was Sindhia, and the palace revolution narrated in these pages cleared the ground for Sindhia's accession to power. Having restored the blinded Shah to titular sovereignty, the great Maratha became the actual director of administration, and under the European officers whom he employed, peace and order returned to the afflicted land. Forty or fifty years ago old men still spoke regretfully of those halcyon days.

The introduction of British rule, with its sure and inflexible methods, had for some time the effect, however unintentional, of interrupting this welfare and producing a contrast. When land became a complete security for debt, and when ancestral acres were brought to the hammer for defaults of Government dues, it was not to be wondered at if the people sighed for the days of Sindhia and his French subordinates. Better times have since ensued; the reign of law has been tempered by sympathetic moderation. But perhaps even now there may be yet something to be learned from the records of a ruder administration more agreeable to the habits of a simple, rural community.[1]

[1] For further particulars refer to *Sindhia* "Rulers of India" Series), Oxford, 1895.

CHAPTER V

Revolution at Dehli—Boigne is recalled by Sindhia—The New Model Army and campaign in Rajputāna—Boigne at Ajmir, Jaipur, and Alwar—Administration at Aligurh—He retires in ill-health, and ultimately returns to Europe—His work at Chambéry, and death.

THE events of 1788 mark the close of a period. Nominally, indeed, no change may have been at first evident. The Shah continued to exercise as much sovereignty as was possible for a blind man; for it is a remarkable instance of the tenacity of Oriental ideas that this apparently hollow semblance still imposed on men's minds. Boigne himself subsequently wrote of this period that "the respect for the race of Timur reigned so strongly that, although the whole of India had withdrawn itself from the Imperial authority, not a prince within its borders claimed sovereign rights; Sindhia shared the feeling, and Shah Alam was always seated on the Moghal throne, while all was done in his name."

Such as this sovereignty may have been, it was the intention of the Maratha chief to shape it to his own use and profit. Though, constitutionally, nothing but a foreigner of distinction called in to administer a disordered State, he was, practically, mayor of the palace, plenipotentiary vicegerent of the Empire, and absolute master of the civil and military resources thereof. In this position he was beset on all sides. At Poona—notwithstanding a certain readiness to help shown in the late war—he was jealously watched by Nana Farnavis,

GENERAL COUNT DE BOIGNE.

(1750–1830.)

the minister of the Peshwa. In Hindustan, although he had got rid of most of his Muslim rivals, he had still to be on guard against Ismail Beg and Najaf Kuli. Most of all had he to apprehend trouble from the Princes of Rajputāna, Jaipur, and the rest; those chieftains—if they could only form a compact and energetic union—could assail his unfinished army with overwhelming force.

The first thing for an able and resolute man so situated was evidently to augment and consolidate his military power; and, as a step in that direction, he forthwith sent a representative to Lucknow to invite the return of his Savoyard friend, to whom he offered something like a blank cheque, in effect the supreme command and free discretion. An offer of renewed employment on these terms Boigne could not refuse. Therefore, having, like a prudent man as he was, wound up his affairs at Lucknow, he left some of his investments in Martin's hands and placed others with good Calcutta firms, proceeding to Mathra about the end of 1789 and at once addressing his whole attention to military reform.

The regulars whom Boigne had formerly raised had become demoralised since his temporary retirement, and their Colonel—a Frenchman of bad character—had deserted with eight months' pay due to the officers and men—a sum equivalent to over £10,000 sterling. The soldiers clamoured for their arrears; Sindhia, on the other hand, was short of temper and disposed to charge the battalions with artillery and horse. The new commander, objecting to this extreme measure, was allowed to deal with the case at his own discretion; and accordingly, by a mixture of threat and promise, prevailed on the men to pile arms and parade bare-handed. They were then formally discharged, half their arrears paid up, and new engagements made with them on altered terms, the officers who had fomented the late ill-conduct being cashiered. Recruiting on a large scale was set on foot in regions where the best material was available; European officers and artillerists were invited, and strong brigades formed. Each brigade was to comprise 4,000 regular infantry (armed with flint muskets and with bayonets), with at least two Christian commissioned officers in each of the battalions; there were to be thirty-six field guns, with a European sergeant-major and five European gunners to each battery; there was also a small siege-train and a body of horse to protect the guns. This force—organised against all Oriental principles—was destined to a short but glorious career, and finally (being augmented by new brigades added from time to time) attained the respectable strength of 68 battalions, 427 guns, and 40,000 horse. Some notice of its later service and ultimate dissolution will be found on a further page.

For the present General de Boigne was at the head of a choice body of troops, chiefly formed of some 16,000 infantry: he was allowed Rs. 10,000 a month for his own pay; and the little army, secure of good treatment, followed its honourable chief under the white cross of Savoy. Lands round Aligurh were assigned for the pay of the officers and men, a promise being recorded that a gratuity should be bestowed on those who were wounded in action, with full pay all the time that they should be in hospital. Invalids were to have pensions on retirement.

Having done all that humanity and wisdom could suggest, the General took the field early in 1790 at the head of his New Model. Some hammering under fire might still be needed, but the steel head was at last fixed firmly on the bamboo lance, as opportunity was soon to show. The tempest that Sindhia had foreseen when he sent his unconditional summons to Boigne at Lucknow was gathering in the south-west, where Ismail's new loyalty was giving way under the combined temptation of his own restless character and the attitude of the Afghans who were beginning to move on the Punjab under Timur Shah, son of their famous leader, Ahmad the Abdālī. Ismail had been put in charge of a district in the Mewāt country between Dehli and the homes of the Rājputs; and it was ostensibly as an ally of these Princes that he now adopted a hostile attitude. No sooner had he raised his standard than disbanded soldiers, the *débris* of the old-fashioned armies, flocked to take service; and it was not long before the mediæval warfare of mounted men-at-arms was to be opposed to artillery and musketry, and squares with flickering bayonet points and flashing fire.

Pending the coming of the Afghans, the Rajas of Jaipur and Jodhpur hurried to the aid of their Muslim ally; and Sindhia sent General de Boigne's legion, with a Maratha force, under two commanders of that race, with orders to prevent the junction, at the same time employing a mixture of threat and promise to the Rajas. Early in May, 1790, the army reached Gwalior, about six weeks after being mobilised at Mathra. The light-armed Maratha horsemen sent out as scouts brought news, on the 10th, that Ismail was strongly entrenched at a place called Pātan, about half-way between Gwalior and Ujain. The Rājputs were at hand, when the Imperial army arrived on the 25th and began to invest the place; but Sindhia's intrigues had already begun to sow mistrust between them and the Beg, and the Rajas took no part in the operations. Had they attacked the rear of the assailants and taken them between two fires, the result might have been different; but with Sindhia the head was always ready to lighten the labour of the hand, and steel was not used when the end could be obtained by silver. Disappointed by his allies and impatient at the confinement and scarcity of the entrenchment, the Beg broke forth on June 19th. With trumpets and kettledrums sounding, clad in chain-mail or plate-armour, the Beg's heavy cavalry charged down, repeatedly breaking the Marathas, and sabring Boigne's gunners at their posts. But the General and his officers kept their heads; the new infantry, reviving the ancient phalanx, resisted all attempts to ride them down with bristling bayonets and well-nourished fire. As the baffled horsemen retired, the General seized the critical moment to advance in line. Placing himself at the head of one of his battalions, he led his men into the entrenchment. There were three lines of defence: the first was carried with the impulse of the advance; the second held out obstinately and did not fall till 8 p.m.; the third yielded an hour later; then the mercenaries ceased their resistance, and the Beg galloped, almost alone, in the direction of Jaipur, where, for a while, he found a grudging refuge. He had lost all his stock-in-trade, one hundred guns, fifty elephants, two hundred colours, and all his baggage; on the following day a great body of his horsemen came over and were taken into the Imperial service. After three days of open trenches the town was taken, and thus the small disciplined force—with but scant aid from the irregulars under Maratha leaders—had broken down the last remnants of the cause of Moghal anarchy. Boigne—who was his own war correspondent—wrote a letter to a Calcutta newspaper in which he estimated the Beg's cavalry at 5,000, and attributed the result of the action to the firmness of his regular battalions, of whom he had with him about 10,000 bayonets, supported by several field-batteries, whose fire preceded his advance. He estimates the loss of his regulars at 592 killed and wounded. He says of himself: "I was on horseback, encouraging our men; thank God, I have realised all the sanguine expectations of Sindhia; the officers in general behaved well; to them I am a great deal indebted for the fortune of the day."

The indolence of the Rājputs has already been noticed, and we have seen how adroitly Sindhia—playing on that and other of their weaknesses—had neutralised their action at a time when it might have done him much mischief. But there was a leading man among them—old Bijai Singh, Maharaja of Mārwar, or Jodhpur—who had a long-standing feud with Sindhia, which he now attempted to make good. The Jaipur Raja Partab Singh had given offence to the Maratha Minister by harbouring Ismail Beg; and Bijai Singh acted on his fears to persuade him into a new combination. But when Sindhia, flushed with his late success, had sent a force into the Jaipur country, though it was only 7,000 strong, that body proved enough to keep the Raja in check; the Beg was persuaded to go off to Multan, and the Savoyard General, having now only Jodhpur to deal with, entered the intervening lands of Ajmir, and captured the town of that name on August 22. Here he received a message from Bijai Singh complimenting him handsomely upon his victory at Pātan, and offering him the town and district of Ajmir as a bribe to induce him to leave the cause of Sindhia and embrace that of the Rājputs. To an ordinary mercenary the proposal might have been temptation; but the General was not a man to imitate the dog in the fable. With grim pleasantry he made answer that his master had already given him both Jodhpur and Jaipur; why should he be content with nothing but Ajmir? About fifteen days later, intelligence arrived that Bijai Singh was advancing to the relief of Tāragarh, the lofty fortress of Ajmir, which the imperialists had invested. Leaving a small force to maintain the blockade of the hill, the General hastened to meet the Jodhpur army, and presently learned that they had encamped under the protecting walls of Mairta, a town some 80 miles north-east of Ajmir. On the evening of September 7 he reconnoitred the position and found the Rāthors—to which great class the Raja and his subjects belonged—strongly entrenched in front of the town, whose walls gave complete cover to the rear of the camp. The ground rose in front, and the strength of the place forbade a rash attack. Gopal Rao, the Maratha General, did indeed urge an immediate onslaught; but Boigne said: "No; the hour is late, the men are tired: let them have a good meal and go to sleep; there will be time enough in the morning."

Profiting by the wise and kindly thought, the imperialists rested that night, while the Rāthors, on their side, spent the hours in rude and loud festivity. In the grey of the morning—when all at last had fallen into the silence of satiety—a French colonel, named Rohan, took out three battalions and crept up the slope, intending to surprise the Rāthors as they lay plunged in half-drunken sleep. But his approach was perceived, and a sufficient number of the garrison were ready to drive out Rohan with loss. Trumpets sounded, the Rāthor horsemen threw on their armour and vaulted to their saddles; pouring out of the camp with reckless ardour, they fell upon the Maratha cavalry, who tried to protect the retreating battalions. The light Southern men and horses scattered before the shock, pursued for miles by Bijai Singh and his cumbrous cavaliers. But these latter, when the enemy had fled, turned their speed-spent chargers to ride back to camp, each side of the valley being by that time lined by the imperialists. The foot were in squares, with field-pieces between; the Rāthors rode down a valley of death. The story went that four thousand saddles were emptied in the ride. Unfatigued and intact, the infantry of the New Model now became assailants in their turn. The battalions, deploying, advanced in line, supported by their field-pieces, and gradually rolled up the motley array of the Rājputs; by 3 p.m. all attempt at opposition had ceased. The whole camp, with munitions of war and vast plunder, rewarded the victors; the conflict of modern warfare with mediæval was decided in favour of science. The hollow-square formation introduced by the Savoyard may have been due to his own initiative or to recollections of the ancient tactics of the Romans; it was now established in Indian fighting, and proved as much of a success against the bold Rājput cavaliers as it was hereafter to become on the more famous field of Mont St. Jean.

The echo of this blow resounded far and wide. Timur Shah heard it in the Khaibar, and held back his barbarian hordes, longing for the loot of India. It reached the Nana at Poona, causing him to redouble his intrigues against his distant but dangerous competitor. Still more did it stimulate the rivalry of Holkar, the immediate neighbour of Sindhia, who resolved to raise a force on the same lines as that which had won such victories for Sindhia. Meanwhile General de Boigne, though much prostrated by months of labour and anxiety in an extreme climate, saw no prospect of repose. Tāragarh, indeed, gave little further trouble, having capitulated in November, after the failure of Bijai Singh to relieve it; but the General marched at once on the enemy's capitals. Jodhpur, Jaipur, and Udaipur all made their submission before the end of the year. To make more effectual the punishment of Jaipur—which had shown signs of meditating a fresh outbreak—the General imposed upon the Raja a fine of seventy lakhs of rupees, in addition to heavy arrears of tribute due to the Imperial exchequer, and marched upon Jaipur to enforce his demand. Partab Singh—the chief in question—saw the uselessness of resistance, after one more lesson, and so, consenting to the terms imposed, appointed a meeting in his capital for the ratification of the agreement. Those who have seen that splendid city may imagine the scene; the unclouded "cold weather" morning with cool breeze and brilliant sun; the wide street lined with orderly spectators; the Maharaja issuing from his lofty palace-gateway, mounted on a richly-caparisoned elephant and followed by a *cortège* of mailed horsemen and many-coloured courtiers; on the other side, the war-worn

General, surrounded by his officers, and escorted by his bodyguard, or *Khās Risāla*. He was welcomed with every mark of respect; the Maharaja took him into his howdah with a public embrace, and they entered the palace together and proceeded to the Durbar hall.

The negotiations being duly ratified, on a basis already settled, the General returned to his camp, and in due time departed on his return to the Duāb. But a strange moment awaited him on the way. As he passed through the small Rājput principality of Macheri—now known as Alwar—he was invited to visit the Rana at his newly-acquired capital, whose name has since been given to the whole State. Here he was received with much ceremony by the Prince, whose friendly sentiments, however, appear to have been by no means universal. As the General was sitting in full Durbar, on the right hand of the Rana, he saw that a follower of the latter was leaning over the back of the chief's chair engaged in earnest conversation with his master in an unknown tongue. The Rana made a gesture of disapprobation, while the vakil—or secretary—of the General turned as pale as his native complexion would allow; the conversation was, however, resumed until the distribution of *pán* and *attar* gave hint that the interview was ended. The Durbar broke up, and as the General rode back to his tent, attended by the vakil, he received from the latter a startling explanation, namely, that the Rana had been considering a proposal for his—the General's—assassination. Boigne was too wise a man to complain, and departed in amity from the Rana's territory, taking his headquarters to Aligurh, the centre of the districts assigned for the pay of his legion. In 1792 the General conducted a brief, but fierce, campaign against Holkar, to be described hereafter, overthrowing his new levies and driving him into Southern Malwa.

This was the termination of the short, but arduous, military labours of the able Savoyard, who was now to be occupied, for the remainder of his stay in India, by the duties of civil administration. During the past two years he had done thoroughly all that had been required of him in the field, having taken two strong fortresses, won several pitched battles, and made his master the lord paramount of a region as wide as France and Germany together. And this he had done, with men hardly equal in native valour to his opponents and very inferior in number, by the force of his own character and the skill of his European subordinates. Of some of these a detailed notice will be taken further on ; here we need only remark that they must have been well chosen and well trained. We will now follow him into civil life, where we shall observe an equal degree of faithful ability.

Indian administration has now become an almost mechanical system, applied with fixed rules, conducted on quasi-scientific principles, and rewarded by considerable success. Peace and order are maintained; pestilence and famine are combated, and the sufferers relieved; justice is attended to, and revenue collected by legal methods. In the time of war and anarchy with which we have been concerned, none of these arrangements were attempted; and now that peace was being restored, all that the best-intentioned men could contemplate was a rough recovery of order in the desolated land.

Aligurh—now the designation of a British District—was a name then used exclusively for a fort hard by the town of Koil, half-way between Agra and Dehli, which had belonged to the late Afrasyăb Khan. Here the General established his headquarters, having his private residence in a house and grounds still known as Sahib-Bagh, on the road between the city and the fort. By virtue of his tenure he was to manage all the estates within the limits of his charge, collecting the revenues, and appropriating to himself any balance which might remain after paying the officers and men of his force, now consisting of 30,000 of all arms, divided into three brigades. In theory the General's salary was Rs. 12,000 a month, with 2 per cent. on the collections. In practice he was Commander-in-Chief of the Imperial army and supreme ruler in all Northern India. For the purposes of this great duty he had a number of European subordinates, brigadiers, and other officers; his old friend, Sangster, being in charge of the gun foundry. In the civil administration there were two departments—the Persian office, where the detailed business was transacted, and the French office, presided over by the General in person; monthly statements were submitted to Sindhia's Council at Dehli.

The manner in which the General carried on these various duties has been set forth by an eye-witness:—

"I have seen him daily and monthly rising with the sun, to survey his factories, review his troops, enlist recruits, direct the vast movements of three brigades (providing for their equipment and supplies), harangue in Durbar, give audience to envoys, administer justice, regulate the civil and revenue affairs, hear letters from different parts, and dictate replies, carry on an intricate diplomatic system, superintend his private trade, examine accounts, direct and move forward a most complex machine" (letter of "Longinus" in the Calcutta *Telegraph*). The same writer adds that the General employed no European to aid him in civil business.

Those who know what it is to work in the trying climate of India can imagine that the combination of so much public and private business in such conditions would tell upon the health of a European now approaching the later period of life. Boigne was now turned of forty years, more than half of which had been passed in toil, danger, and anxiety; he was very rich, as riches were then considered, and his thoughts, no doubt, often turned to home and rest. On February 12, 1794, he lost his generous master, Mahadaji Sindhia, who died suddenly while on a visit to Poona. The estates and offices of the deceased devolved on his grandnephew, Daulat Rao, a young man of very inferior character and capacity, who remained in the Deccan, leaving the affairs of Hindustan to be managed by the General. That officer accordingly soon became the centre of intrigue. Offers on behalf of the blind old Emperor, and contrary offers from the new Shah of Cabul, failed to move him. For he declared that it was not for him to pronounce upon the destinies of the Dehli throne ; he was in the service of the house of Sindhia ; if he ceased to serve that house he would cease to serve at all. The young Vicegerent was unwilling to part with so faithful and valued a subordinate, but the General became more and more bent on leaving India, till towards the end of 1795 it appeared that, unless he did so at once, his life would not be prolonged. Thus he at length obtained indefinite leave of absence and left Aligurh for ever.

In February, 1796, he marched out at the head of his bodyguard, and, after some months of vain struggle for recovery at Lucknow, finally reached Calcutta. During the General's stay at Lucknow[1] the Nawab made an unavailing attempt to obtain possession of the splendid corps which accompanied the invalid—a body of six hundred Persian troopers, superbly armed, mounted, and equipped, with a hundred camel-men on high-bred animals, and a small battery of light guns, the whole of the property being owned by himself. It was eventually acquired for the East India Company by the then Governor-General, who paid a handsome sum to Boigne and gave liberal terms of engagement to the men. In January, 1797, the General, having wound up all his Indian affairs, finally left the port of Calcutta on board the Danish vessel *Cronberg*, com-

[1] For some account of the General's health and of his uncertainty hile at Lucknow, v. Appendix.

manded by Captain Tennant. A Calcutta journalist bore the following testimony to his character : "In his military capacity he softened, by means of an admirable perseverance, the ferocious nature of the Marathas. He submitted to the discipline and civilisation of Europe soldiers who till then had been regarded as barbarians."

He was not only the greatest soldier of his class, but by far the most distinguished by benevolence and general ability.

CHAPTER VI

General de Boigne in retirement—His good deeds and recognition by his King and country—Death and burial.

WHEN General de Boigne quitted the shores of India he may well have looked upon himself as one of whom it might be said, "His warfare is accomplished." Although his actual service in the field had lasted only between five and six years, he had assuredly done a great work. In the civil department in which he had been exclusively engaged since he brought back his victorious brigades from Rajputāna, he had laboured for an even shorter period; yet it is the recorded opinion of a distinguished historian that he "made it possible for Sindhia to rule in Hindustan, at the same time that he controlled the councils of Poona. . . . It was Boigne who introduced into the North-West Provinces the germs of that civil administration which the English have since successfully developed."[1] Surely a very remarkable record for any man to show, even if that man had been habituated and practised in either military or civil action, still more when he was a foreigner and little more than an amateur in both. He might well solace the tardy hours of a voyage round the Cape by anticipations of repose in a brief obscurity; as a matter of fact, a future of over thirty years was still before him, filled with honourable and useful occupation.

The passage was not, however, a long one, as things

[1] Malleson, *Final French Struggles.*

then went; the *Cronberg* arrived in the Thames before the end of 1797, which had been a year of some excitement in London. The news had just arrived of the death of his old mistress, the Czarina Catherine—full to the last of those designs against Persia and India in which he had once been almost led to aid her efforts. The Spanish Government had declared war against the British, and the men of the Royal Navy were choosing that moment to break into open mutiny, blockading the mouth of the river and actually detaining merchant ships. The General, however, found order restored and navigation set free. He was so welcomed in London that he made that foggy capital his social centre for some years. By and by, as things settled down in France, he transferred his headquarters to Paris, where he married the daughter of a returned *émigré*, the Marquis d'Osmond; but the marriage was not a success, and the General went on to his native land, where the King made him a Count and where he settled with his son. Whatever may have been his disillusions, it does not appear that they ever induced him to regret India, or to show the very least inclination to return to the land of his glory. In 1799 Sindhia wrote him a letter in which he courteously replied to one in which the General had sought the aid of his former master in some matters of private business: "Since it has pleased God," wrote the chief, "since it has pleased the Universal Physician to restore to you the blessing of health, and having regard to our jealous impatience to see you again, it is your bounden duty no more to prolong your stay in Europe, but to appear before the Presence with all possible despatch . . . without your wisdom the execution of the greatest projects is entirely suspended." Come out, in fact, at once, and by Bombay!

So wrote Sindhia, with much more to the same effect, but the bird was flown, and too wise to be caught by any chaff that could be thrown out from the Poona Chancery where, indeed, matters were ripening in which our wary adventurer would not have engaged with a light heart. Of these we shall get a glimpse in a later chapter.

Meanwhile we notice the General, not yet separated from his wife, frequenting society at Paris and rumoured —so Wellesley wrote—as much consulted by a still abler adventurer than himself, the General Bonaparte. After that great soldier had become Emperor of the French, and scourge of Europe, General de Boigne characterised his system of politics as "an usurpation abounding in iniquities"; nevertheless he may possibly have been asked for information about India at an earlier period and have given it, as the lawyers say, without prejudice.

In any case, he certainly left France for good, but as certainly approved of the Restoration, which relieved Savoy and other minor Powers of much unpleasant pressure. Louis XVIII. showed him attention, making him Maréchal du Camp in the French army, and giving him the Grand Cross of the Legion of Honour.

He continued, however, to be a good citizen of the small provincial capital in which he had first seen the light. Thus, so late as 1822, he delivered an address to the Chambéry Municipal Council from which the following passages may be extracted to our advantage:—

"If Divine Providence has deigned to crown with success the military career that I had embraced and long followed, it has at the same time loaded me with the gifts of fortune beyond my feeble talents, my endeavours, I will even say, my desires. Inheriting nothing from my father, owing all to God, I see my duty of recognition in seeking to assuage the sufferings of humanity. . . . Accordingly I hesitate no longer to put in execution my long-studied project for the foundation of institutions for the relief of misery and for the benefit of my fellow-citizens.

"Trusting, gentlemen, to your public spirit, I flatter myself that we may succeed in bringing into this town many beneficial changes whereby it may become more healthy, more agreeable to all, and at the same time more especially advantageous to those who, borne down by infirmities, too often perish for want of timely aid after enduring remediable trouble."

The Council promptly voted a suitable reply to this address, and gratefully accepted the truly liberal proposals of "General Count de Boigne." Nor was the national Government backward in acknowledgment; by order of the King, the bust of the munificent "Nabab" was executed in marble for the public library, and he was made Lieutenant-General of the Kingdom and Grand Cross of the Order of SS. Maurice and Lazarus.[1]

This was indeed a "Happy Warrior," who was not content with an unprecedented prosperity so long as he had not made his fellow-citizens partakers of it. Among his benefactions to his native place have been enumerated :—

Extension of the Hôtel-Dieu Hospital by additional wards for sick paupers; an almshouse for forty aged persons of either sex; an endowed mendicity depôt for one hundred paupers, with an asylum for pauper lunatics; a supplementary infirmary for those afflicted with infectious disorders, and another for travellers; these first, for the helpless and ruined adult. But the young were also cared for: there was an endowment for placing in life deserving children of both sexes, and an exhibition in the Royal College. A new Capuchin Church was built; the theatre was repaired at a cost of 60,000 francs; a new street, with a colonnade, was opened through the whole breadth of the town; two old streets were widened, and much-needed improvements were made to the public library and the Town Hall; finally, annuities were founded for the Academic Society, the volunteer corps, and the fire brigade.

[1] For a notice of the General about this time see Tod's *Rajasthan*, i. 765: Colonel Tod visited Chambéry in 1826, and saw him there.

Thus no class of society, no department of life, lacked the attention of the wise and benevolent veteran; and Chambéry might have said of him: If you would seek his monument, look round. What she did say was much to the same effect; the address of the municipality closed with these words:—

"You have foreseen all sorrows, to provide for each a cure; the unfortunate find in you support at every instant of their lives. Age reposes by the side of the tomb; and youth gains new wings for its ardour, deriving from a strong, pious, and skilful education the conservative principles of human society; while your example inspires the fire of the noblest enterprises."

In the midst of these good works age stole slowly on the veteran. Colonel Tod, the historian of his old enemies in Rajputāna, visiting him in 1826, thought him still vigorous. But in the following years his strength began to fail, and at last yielded to one of those light touches to which an octogenarian must be always liable. On the 25th of June, 1830, the *Journal de Savoie* announced his death as having taken place four days before. For two days every shop and place of business in the city remained closed; the bells tolled unceasingly from every steeple while the body lay in state in the Cathedral, watched by the "Company of Noble Knights." The funeral was followed by the royal household; the town-guard; the Academic Society; the Chamber of Commerce; the directors of the Hospitals; the magistrates, aldermen, and notables of the city; fifty of the General's tenant farmers, and a crowd of workmen, together with columns of troops, their bands playing funeral marches; closed by numbers of clergy and the poor.

A few days later, the Academy offered a prize for the best biography of the deceased, which was, in due course, awarded to his son, Count Charles de Boigne. At the same time the Town Council made two public fountains in further commemoration, thus giving the dead benefactor a fresh means of that well-doing which had occupied his latest living thoughts.

Such was the retirement of this great Savoyard, at a time when his British contemporaries were spending their ill-gotten gains in idle ostentation and political corruption; "raising," as has been said, "nothing but the price of fresh eggs and rotten boroughs."

In person General de Boigne was tall and handsome; the portrait prefixed to the Memoir by his son shows a fine head and projecting brow. The eyes and nose also are strong and prominent; the shaven lips are firm and not too thin; the lower jaw and chin are boldly squared. Like his great co-eval and patron, Warren Hastings, he was of temperate and scholarly habits, and well-versed in Latin literature; he wrote and read several modern languages with ease and correctness; his conversation, according to contemporaneous witnesses, was witty and graceful. Colonel Francklin, an able British officer of those days, and at the time one of the most popular writers on Indian subjects, has recorded strong testimony in favour of his accomplishments.

It must be evident that, with the one exception of his not very successful matrimonial experiment, General de Boigne is a singular example of human possibility.

CHAPTER VII

Records of the New Model—Chevalier du Drenec and the fight at the Pass of Lakhain—Charge of Rāthors at Sanganir—Michel Raymond—The Battle of Kardla—The Nizam's regular troops disbanded by order of Mornington—The brothers Filose.

We have seen, in observing the military career of General de Boigne, how the secular contest between cavalry and infantry developed in India, where the mediæval ideas of warfare lingered after they had been dispelled in more progressive regions. The tactics which had been originated in Europe by Edward III. proceeded on the experience which showed that a man is a better fighter than a horse. If a line of spikes holds firm, and is supported by a continuous discharge of missiles, the horse will not charge home, let the courage of the rider be ever so high. But, to produce these conditions in the infantry, the foot soldiers must be self-respecting men, thoroughly well-disciplined and commanded. We have seen what, in the opinion of contemporaneous journalists, had been the moral evolution of the Indian soldier in the New Model; it is therefore proper that we should now endeavour to learn something of the subordinate officers by whose help that result had been obtained. In this attempt we can fortunately command the aid of a competent writer who was himself a member of the force. In treating of General de Boigne, the testimony of a newspaper correspondent who used the signature of "Longinus" was cited above; the true designation of whom was Louis Ferdinand Smith, Major in the army of Sindhia.

The account of some of the more remarkable of these officers of fortune published by Major Smith was brought out by subscription in Calcutta, without any date upon the title-page, but apparently about the year 1804, and subsequently reprinted in London. Many of the names on the subscription list are those of men who afterwards found honourable mention in Anglo-Indian history, among them being those of Sir John Anstruther, the then Chief Justice; of Sir George Barlow, afterwards Governor of Madras; of Becher, Boileau, Colvin, familiar as founders of well-known Indian clans; of others of like type; of General Ochterlony; and of the Marquess Wellesley, who at that time ruled the Indian Empire as then constituted. The little work has only some ninety pages, but it is a workmanlike piece, illustrated with well-drawn plans of battles, and it bears the title, *A Sketch of the Rise, Progress, and Termination of the Regular Corps formed and commanded by Europeans in the Service of the Native Princes of India.* It is to the information which it gives that we shall be indebted for almost all that we can learn upon the subject in the way of biographic fact in this chapter.

Most of the officers referred to were Frenchmen who had originally come out to Pondichéri with Lally and been left to seek their fortune after the collapse of the French enterprise in 1760. Of such were Médoc (of whom some account has been given already), as also Martin, Sombre, St. Frais; probably Du Drenec and Perron; certainly Law.[1] What was to be said of these also has been said, excepting Perron and Du Drenec. At a later date appeared the Hessings—Hollanders; the Filoses—Neapolitans; and, of Britons and Anglo-Indians, the Skinners, Gardner, Shepherd, Sutherland, Davies, Dodd, Vickers, Bellasis, and the brothers Smith. Most of these were, sooner or later, in Sindhia's service; but the

[1] For a further notice of these men about 1764, see Broome's *Bengal Army*, p. 419.

greatest of all, George Thomas, fought for his own hand, like Hal of the Wynd, and his exploits are accordingly recorded separately here.

Of the Chevalier du Drenec there is not very much to note. His very name is uncertain, one calling him Dudernek, another Dodernaigue, according to phonetic interpretation of native usage. He seems to have belonged to an ancient Breton family—now extinct—known in provincial history as "Du Drenek-Keroulas"; he did not enter life in the army, but came to India as *enseigne-de-vaisseau* (midshipman) about 1773. French power and influence in the Indian seas were at the lowest at that moment, when the Treaty of Paris (1763) had indeed "restored Pondichéri to France, but it was a Pondichéri dismantled, beggared, bereft of all her influence. During the fifteen years which followed . . . Pondichéri had been forced to remain a powerless spectator of her rival on Indian soil."[1] Not finding encouragement in so depressed a service, the young sailor quitted his ship and made his way up the country, where he joined his countryman, Médoc, and they both engaged in the Imperial service under Mirza Najaf. On the departure of Médoc, the Chevalier also vanished from the scene in Hindustan; whether in a return to Europe or in wanderings about India, we have no information. At length, in 1791, we hear of him as retained to raise a body of foot by Tukaji Holkar, then engaged in an attempt to emulate the success of Madahaji Sindhia. The force of Du Drenec consisted of four battalions; but before it had been completely trained, it was unfortunate enough to encounter a strong detachment under General de Boigne in person. Almost everything was against the young legion: the fame and prestige of the enemy's leader, their own inexperience, and the smallness of their numbers. But Holkar had political reasons for desiring to invade the territories of his rival. In June, 1792,

[1] Malleson's *Final French Struggles*, pp. 3, 4.

Sindhia had set out on his last journey to Poona, where he became engaged in a struggle for favour with the astute Brahman, Nana Farnavis; and he had sent for a strong bodyguard of regulars, weakening his local army by 10,000 of his best men. The moment seemed to Holkar full of promise. Summoning Ismail Beg from his temporary retirement, he hurled his cavalry on northern Malwa, the new legion, with a strong artillery, acting as the nucleus of the force.

The first counter-stroke was delivered at a strong place called Kanaund, in the northern part of the arid tract that lies between the capital and the borders of Hariana. Here the client of Mirza Najaf, who has been already mentioned as a converted Hindu called Najaf Kuli Khan, had just died in a stronghold of earth faced with stone, among sand-hills and low growths of tamarisks, where his widow—a sister of the late Ghulām Kādar—continued to reside. Ismail Beg—who was an old ally of the family—flew to the aid of his deceased friend's sister; and a column under Colonel Perron marched to besiege the place. Some account of the siege will be found in the story of Perron later on; at present we have only to notice that Holkar's army advanced at its best pace in the hope of relieving Kanaund and raising the siege. Boigne, bent on frustrating this design, came against them; and the two forces met in September, 1792, at Lakhairi, on the road leading from Ajmir. The Marathas were posted on ground well chosen, the guns and infantry being on the crest of a pass; a marsh covered the front, the sides being flanked by deep jungle and trees, and protected by no less than 30,000 Maratha horsemen. The action that ensued was considered by Boigne the severest in which he was ever engaged. As he led up his battalions he was exposed to a terrific fire from Holkar's batteries, and his own guns, on the support of which he had relied, met with unexpected misfortune. The marsh impeded their progress, and, as they advanced slowly under the enemy's fire, they became rapidly disabled. First, a tumbril was hit by a hostile ball and exploded; this explosion communicated itself to the next carriage. In a short time a dozen ammunition-wagons were on fire, scattering around the whole of their contents. With rapid instinct Holkar caught the flying instant, and sought to charge the guns by extricating his squadrons from the protection of the jungle. But even in that terrible crisis the influence of discipline prevailed; the seasoned battalions of the enemy breasted the hill in face of all obstacles, firing from flank and rear at the encumbered cavalry. Maratha horsemen were always better at scouting than in a pitched battle. Ismail, with his men-at-arms, might have led an effectual charge, but Ismail was engaged elsewhere. As Holkar and his light horse withered under the fire of Boigne's musketeers, they were charged by the Moghal cavalry, few in number, but superior in equipment and weight. The whole force was quickly dispersed. Delivered from these dangers, the column resumed its advance up the pass, held tenaciously by the batteries and battalions of Du Drenec. Raw levies as they were, they did credit to their leader. The European officers fell at their posts —with the exception of their leader; the men were shot or bayoneted where they stood; thirty-eight guns were lost. It was the first encounter between two bodies imbued with the same discipline; the scale had been turned by the inefficiency of Holkar's horsemen; but Du Drenec had covered himself with whatever glory was obtainable in such fields.

Escaping from this slaughter, which ceased on the cessation of resistance, our adventurer did nothing more for some time, beyond taking part in the campaign in the Deccan which ended with the battle of Kardla (1795). As we have no particulars of his conduct on that occasion, the description may be postponed till we come to notice the career of Raymond, who commanded on the side of the Nizam. The next time of meeting the Chevalier is in 1799, when he was on the winning side at the battle of Sanganir, though temporarily involved in a catastrophe that—as at Lakhairi—left him almost sole survivor of his force. This was the last (or almost the last) of the fights between the Princes of Rajputāna and the head of the house of Sindhia—once quieted by Boigne, as we have seen. That able officer was now in retirement—we have noted the new Sindhia's letter vainly attempting his recall. The chief command in Hindustan had devolved on a native General called Lakwa Dada, the chief being away at Poona, and Jaipur joined to Jodhpur in a renewed rebellion. So formidable appeared this outbreak that Ambaji Ainglia was deputed to the Dada's aid, taking with him a strong brigade of disciplined foot commanded by Du Drenec. The whole force consisted of six brigades of infantry with the due artillery, 20,000 Maratha horsemen, and a motley contingent of irregular spearmen on foot. On the Rājput side was an infantry far inferior; but there was also a noble force of 50,000 heavy cavalry, the fighting Rāthors of Marwar (Jodhpur), of whom we have already heard. Sanganir, where the encounter took place, is the name of a small village situated on the sandy plain west of Jaipur city; and here the troops of Sindhia attacked the Rājputs one March morning in 1799. But the Rāthor horsemen were on the alert; and, under command of Siwai Singh—a henchman of the Jodhpur Raja—charged furiously down on the intruders, the brigade of Du Drenec, who had endeavoured to surprise their morning slumbers. The scene of Mairta was now reproduced, with very important variations. More than 10,000 in number, the Rāthor cavaliers trotted their horses out of the lines, while the battle began to rage in other quarters. Du Drenec prepared to receive the charges with squares formed and field-pieces belching grape from the intervals. But the Rāthors would take no denial, the trot became a gallop as they drew near, and the noise of their onward rush was heard—says an eye-witness—above all the roar of the battle. Regardless of the grape-shot, riding over fifteen hundred of their own front ranks laid low by the fire of Du Drenec's infantry and field-pieces, they pressed on with increased momentum. Neither the fire of the grape-loaded cannon nor the glitter of the bristling bayonets availed to check the charge. Like a storm-wave it passed over the brigade, leaving scarcely a vestige of life in its track. Du Drenec was flung under a gun-carriage; almost all his Europeans lost their lives on the spot. Nevertheless the day of heavy cavalry had departed; science and discipline asserted themselves in spite of headlong valour; the Răjputs were finally put to flight with almost incredible carnage; that single action decided the campaign.[1]

Du Drenec—perhaps in consequence of these defeats—left the service of Holkar and joined Perron at Aligurh, where his house is still in existence and serves as the Court House of the District Judge. In September, 1803 (when Lake advanced from Cawnpore), Du Drenec was absent, having been posted at Poona in command of 5,000 men. Ordered to Hindustan, he started to obey; but by the time of his arrival at Mathra he heard of the fall of Aligurh and Dehli, and of the march on Agra, while he found his troops suspicious of their European officers. In these trying circumstances the Chevalier adopted the wisest course open to him, surrendering to Colonel Vandeleur, of the 8th Dragoons, in company with Major Smith — our author — and another white officer. The British authorities gladly permitted them to go into private life, with all that belonged to them. Du Drenec seems to have settled in the country, for Smith (in the book referred to) mentions him as having

[1] This account is condensed from that given by Colonel Skinner, C.B., who was present with Sindhia's army.

been thirty years in India and being still there while he (Smith) was writing.

In the battle of Kardla—to be noted presently—where the power of the Deccan Moghals was temporarily broken by their Maratha neighbours—the victorious side, on which Du Drenec fought, was opposed by an equally brave and more distinguished French officer. Although the Nizam's Regulars were unable to achieve success, the fault was by no means theirs; and their commander was a meritorious man, said to be still commemorated by the natives of those regions.

In what line of life Michel Raymond was bred is not recorded, but he was a native of France and came out to Pondichéri in a mercantile firm. In 1778 Great Britain declared war with the French Government, who were openly abetting the revolted Colonies in North America. On receipt of the news the authorities of Fort St. George sent a force to besiege Pondichéri, which capitulated after a respectable defence; and Raymond (with a nephew of Count Lally, and other adventurous men) repaired to Mysore, where he enrolled himself in the service of Haidar Ali, the usurper of that State, and irreconcilable enemy of the British. In 1783 the famous Patissier, known in Indian history as "Marquis de Bussy-Castelnau," had returned, under orders from Louis XVI., to the country where he had won so much distinction twenty years before; and he was now, with shattered health and a mind enfeebled by years and slothful living, engaged in a hopeless contest with Sir Eyre Coote. Raymond's old employer, Haidar, having just died, the French adventurer was free to accept a post on Bussy's staff; and, on Bussy's death two years later, Raymond betook himself to the capital of the Nizam, where he obtained a high command. Up to this time Raymond had won no great distinction as a soldier; but he had temper, character, and talent, all which had become known and raised him to a similar position at Haidarabad to that which Boigne was soon to create for himself in the North. He gradually got together a respectable force of 15,000 regular infantry, with no less than 124 superior officers, all of European blood.

To mature this force was the work of seven or eight years, during which Raymond worked with very great success. At length, on the 10th of March, 1795, he marched from Bidar, with the army of the Nizam, mustering 70,000 irregular infantry, supported by 20,000 horsemen and a due proportion of artillery, under command of French officers. To meet this invasion the Peshwa had assembled a force estimated at 100,000 of all arms, including ten of Sindhia's trained battalions under Perron, four under Du Drenec, contributed by Holkar, with other similar contingents commanded, respectively, by Hessing, Filose, and Boyd, of all of whom we shall presently have a word or two to say. The armies were thus equally matched in all respects; nearly equal in numbers and organisation; each animated by the presence of good European officers. The encounter occurred at a place two marches to the south-west of Poona, which city would be at the mercy of the Moghals if they could prevail over the Maratha army. This latter was encamped on the slopes of the Purindha pass, the artillery being skilfully disposed on the heights above. The Moghals had the disadvantage of having to advance from lower ground, occupying as they did the plain between the pass and the village of Kardla; nevertheless there was sufficient ground for cavalry, by a bold use of which the Moghals drove back the Maratha right; Raymond's battalions, on the other side, advanced steadily under a heavy fire from Perron's guns, and the fight developed into a duel between the two Frenchmen, one endeavouring to storm the pass, the other determined to defend it. But the Moghal horse had fled in wild confusion under a tempest from the Maratha rocket-batteries; and the aged Nizam, who—

after the Asiatic manner—trusted only to his cavalry, insisted on retreat. Raymond's escort being essential to the safety of the Prince, he was obliged to retire, and the day was lost, although the retirement was effected in good order and there was no pursuit.

Raymond's next service was in suppressing the rebellion of the Nizam's heir-apparent, Mirza Ali Jah, who seized upon the fortifications of Bidar, and collected a following of disaffected chiefs and disbanded soldiers which Raymond easily dispersed in the month of June of the same year (1795). From that time he pursued his life of useful and faithful labour until his death, on the 25th of March, 1798, in time to be spared the pain of seeing the abolition of the trained force for which he had done so much. For the times were critical, and Lord Mornington, who had just assumed the office of Governor-General, which he was afterwards to render so illustrious under his later title of "Marquis Wellesley," had a grave combination to encounter. In the Punjab was an invading army of Afghans under Zaman Shah; in Mysore was the valiant Tippu, who had succeeded to the usurped power and to the anti-British policy of his father, Haidar. In Hindustan a French General has taken the place of the friendly Savoyard; in the Deccan an unscrupulous Maratha traitor held power at Poona and the Nizam was vacillating at Haidarabad. Tippu was in correspondence with Zaman Shah and harbouring French adventurers at Seringapatam. Perron had sent a mission to the young General Bonaparte, then on the eve of starting for Egypt. It was impossible that the British in India could render theirs the paramount power or could consolidate their Empire, so long as French officers were predominant in the chief native courts. It is an injustice to ascribe to Mornington—as is often done by injudicious admirers—a conscious plan of conquest. Judged by his own sayings and doings, his was a policy of peace and order. He wrote of "our alacrity to resist aggression and to punish all the Principals and Accomplices of unjust attacks on a Government uniting moderation with energy and equally *determined to respect the just rights of other States.*" Nor was his conduct inconsistent: only that the presence and influence of French Republicans from Seringapatam to Dehli was felt to be totally incompatible with the expressed intentions.

The Nizam was the least formidable of all the country powers, and his regulars under Raymond had never given the British Government trouble, while their officers had for years lived side by side with ours in neighbourly comradeship. But there is no place for sentiment in such a policy as Mornington's. A few weeks after Raymond's death, his master was compelled to execute a treaty with the Company's Government including a clause for the disbanding of the force. As there was to be a "Haidarabad Contingent" under British command, this clause virtually implied nothing but the discharge of the French officers. The practical part of the affair was entrusted to Captain (afterwards Sir John) Malcolm, who displayed on that occasion much of the combined tact and firmness which afterwards—with some allowances for a too genial nature—made him the most famous of all the great soldier-diplomatists of the Anglo-Indian service. The French officers were sent to Europe at the public cost.

So ended the work of Michel Raymond; but his memory remained. Colonel Malleson, who on the spot collected and digested almost all the facts, thus concludes his remarks: "No European of mark who preceded him, no European of mark who followed him in India, ever succeeded in gaining to such an extent the love, the esteem, the admiration of the natives. The grandsons of the men who loved him then revere him now: the hero of the grandfathers is the model warrior of the grandchildren. Round his tomb at the present day there flock still young men and maidens listening to the tales told by wild dervishes of the great deeds and lofty aspirations of the paladin to whom their sires devoted their fortunes and their lives." [1]

The officers of Boigne's brigades, superior as they may have been in military experience, were in no case the equals of Raymond in ability or personal character; and —with the single exception of the General himself—left no memory among the people. The character of the French officers also changed about the time of Boigne's retirement; whether the vicissitudes of the Revolution had anything to do with the fact or whether it was due to the constantly increasing supply of British-born adventurers, it would be hopeless to inquire and impossible to determine.

We have, however, a curious testimony to the low esteem into which the French adventurers had fallen in papers found in Tippu's office at the taking of Seringapatam; the character and conduct of the foreign officers of Sombre's brigade will be shown in the succeeding chapter. General de Boigne is only known to have employed two Italian officers; and their record is far from exemplary. These were two Neapolitans, brothers named Filose, who were in command of fourteen battalions at Poona when the elder Sindhia died and remained there for some time afterward, as the bravos of local politics. Michele, the elder, was driven from the service for a treacherous outrage on the old Minister, Nana Farnavis, in 1797. His brigade was divided, one half being assigned to his brother Fidele, who (in spite of his name) entered into an intrigue with his employer's chief opponent in 1801. His treason being detected, he retired to Ujain, where he terminated an inglorious career by cutting his throat. Other unworthy successors of Law, Médoc, and Du Drenec will be noticed in the account of General Perron, the best of the new series.

[1] *Final French Struggles in India*, London, 1884. See also Grant Duff's *Mahrattas*, ii. 281.

CHAPTER VIII

Origins of George Thomas and the Begum Sombre—The Begum's marriage and consequent misfortunes—First attempts of Thomas as independent leader—Change in character of French adventurers—Ruined condition of Hindustan.

WE now come to a very different case: that of a man of humble origin indeed, but one who only needed conduct to enable him to fill a splendid place in the Anglo-Indian pantheon: the old saying of Juvenal illustrated—"Nullum numen abest si sit prudentia."

George Thomas was a native of Ireland though not, perhaps, of purely Hibernian origin, having been bred in Tipperary where a number of Cromwell's Ironsides had been settled in the seventeenth century. Coming to Madras as quartermaster of a man-of-war in the squadron of Sir Edward Hughes, he deserted in 1782, after the four inconclusive engagements fought in those waters between that Admiral and the Bailli de Suffren. After an obscure period of adventure among the Poligars of the Carnatic he appeared at Sardhana, where the relict of Sombre, known in Indian history as the "Begum Sombre," was holding the fief that had been allotted to that General for the maintenance of his legion in the Imperial service then administered by Sindhia. That remarkable woman was destined to have a considerable influence on the career of Thomas, and no picture of the Anarchy that preceded the British occupation of Hindustan could have any pretence to completeness if it did not contain some notice of her singular fortunes.

Sombre, as we have seen, died at Agra in 1778; he was buried under a masonry canopy which is still to be seen in the Catholic cemetery there, his tomb bearing a Portuguese inscription. He left an insane wife and a son still in early childhood, and his fief was assumed, under an authoritative grant, by a favourite slave-girl whom he had purchased at Dehli; she is believed to have been born at Kotana in the Meerut District, and to have been of Arab origin. Although usually regarded as Walter Reinhardt's (Sombre's) relict, it is quite clear that she could not have been married with the rites of the Romish Church, seeing that he was a married man. Even if not yet a member of the Church, she was dealing with a man who was one.

The new Princess was—in any case—of Moslem birth but apparently found it convenient to conform to the creed of her protector, three years after whose death she was baptized along with her stepson (May 7, 1781). She then settled with her brigade at Sardhana, a village near Meerut; and it was there that Thomas entered the service in which he soon attained great distinction. In the spring of the terrible year 1788—famous for the temporary triumph of Ismail Beg and Ghulām Kādar Khan. with the horrors which ensued—the Emperor Shah Alam undertook a futile expedition into the country between Dehli and Ajmir. Thomas accompanied in command of the Sardhana contingent and the Begum joined personally in the expedition. On the 5th of April the army halted to besiege Gokalgurh in what is now the District of Gurgaon. This was a strong place occupied by the converted Rājput, Najaf Kuli, already more than once mentioned; and he had gone into rebellion against the decrepit Government, for which conduct it was desired to bring him to account. On the arrival of the Imperial forces the garrison made an immediate sortie, and the Moghals, taken by surprise, were thrown into great confusion. The assailants penetrated to the centre of the camps, near where the Imperial standard had been erected in front of the tent in which the Emperor was reposing. With rapid resolution the Begum hastened up in her palanquin, attended by Thomas, with three battalions of infantry and a field-piece. Deploying, as best he might, and with his cannon manned by European gunners in the centre, the Irish seaman covered the Imperial abode and pelted the rebel horsemen with musketry and grape. Surprised in their turn by so unexpected a reception, the enemy wavered, hung back, and, when a body of Moghal cavalry had come to the spot, were finally repulsed. The Emperor's person was saved; the defence so boldly begun turned into a rout; the place was carried in the rush of the pursuit and the credit of the day was justly awarded to the valorous lady. In the Durbar that was held in the afternoon the Begum was publicly thanked by the Sovereign and honoured with the title of *Zeb-un-nissa* ("Glory of the Sex"), which she ever afterward continued to bear, along with that of "Joanna Nobilis," bestowed on her by the Church at her baptism.

At this time the Begum was still in the prime of life and, according to the description given at a later period by Thomas, was distinguished by a plump figure and fair complexion with large and lively eyes. Though of pure Muslim blood and always dressing in native costume, she had partially adopted European manners and sat at table unveiled. It was natural that a lady so rich and otherwise gifted should receive admiration from the soldiers-of-fortune by whom she was surrounded and perhaps be the object of selfish aspiration.

The brigade at this time consisted of five battalions, a regiment of Moghal horse, with forty pieces of artillery; it contained three hundred Europeans, of whom the majority were gunners, and the officers not perhaps all of much higher social standing.

After the Emperor's return from his abortive campaign

—for the capture of Gokalgurh was the only success—he returned to Dehli and there underwent the terrible experiences of which mention has been already made. The Begum took her brigade to his help and once succeeded for a few weeks in delivering the poor old man from his tormentors. But when she had departed, Ghulām Kādar returned, accompanied by Ismail Beg and a force too strong to be successfully attacked; and the Imperial tragedy went forward. For the next four years no Sardhana record is forthcoming; but it is possible that Thomas was a candidate for the lady's favour though ousted by the superior attractions of a rival. In any case it is certain that in 1792 Thomas left the service and that the Begum, about that time, bestowed her hand on M. Levassoult, a French officer whom she had put at the head of the brigade. She was married by the rites of the Romish Church, unfortunately in a somewhat clandestine manner; but the bridegroom was wise enough to provide two witnesses, countrymen and brother-officers, named Bernier and Saleur.

Thomas, meanwhile, had quitted the Sardhana service and betaken himself to Anupshahr, where he became the guest of the officers of a British Frontier Force which was maintained there under a treaty with the Nawab of Oudh, in whose territory it lay. The place is now a decayed town on the right bank of the Ganges, which eats it year by year; but the numerous graves (from which all the memorial tombstones have long since disappeared) are a silent testimony of its former importance.

Settled here under the protection of Colonel MacGowan, the British Brigadier, Thomas lived a pleasant life so long as his savings held out. Then, under the pressure of necessity, he was compelled to look about for means of livelihood. He accordingly took measures to acquaint the neighbouring nobility and gentry that he was prepared to execute orders for rapine and slaughter, and ere long obtained an engagement from a Maratha chief, one

Appa Khandi Rao, who had been in charge of the Gwalior District but whom Sindhia had lately for some reason or other seen fit to discharge. This chieftain was now preparing to take part in the game of grab that was already—had he known it—almost on the point of abolition; and he engaged Thomas and his personal following, with orders to raise a small body of horse and one thousand foot, the reversion of certain lands—to be occupied hereafter—being assigned as a material guarantee for the equipment and pay of the little legion. The country thus bestowed was not only not transferable to the possession of the donee, it did not even belong to the donor. It belonged, in a strictly legal sense, to the sovereign—that is, to the Emperor at Dehli; in another derivative, but equally lawful, way it belonged to the Alwar Raja, to whom it had been assigned by Imperial patent; finally, it was actually in the possession of the Mewāti tribe. Of these last the memoir of Thomas only deigns to observe that "when a large force was sent against them, they usually took shelter in the mountains; but when the force was inferior in numbers, by uniting they proved victorious." By this unreasonable contumacy the Mewātis of these parts had incurred the displeasure of Appa Khandi who, conceiving himself entitled to their surplus produce, availed himself of the Irish sailor's help to bring them to a better frame of mind. Agreeing to balance accounts every six months and furnished with two guns and a store of ammunition, George departed to kill the bear whose skin had thus been conferred upon him.

While Mr. Thomas (as his biographer is always careful to call him) was thus whiling away the shining hours, his former Princess was going through a stimulating experience.

Mention has been made of the rough and lawless character of too many of the late General Sombre's officers; the greater number of them, indeed, were most illiterate ruffians who bitterly resented the airs and graces of their new master, by whose wish they were excluded from the dinner table of the Begum and generally kept at a distance. They affected also to be scandalised at what they, perhaps honestly, regarded as a mere intrigue *à la Catherine Deux;* and in all their discontents they were egged on by taunts and promises from a scheming rival. This was Aloysius Balthazar Reinhardt, son of the deceased General by the Muslim wife, whose crazy brain he would seem to have inherited. This youth had for the last few years been residing at Dehli, wearing native costume and bearing native titles, being known there as "Nawab Zafaryab Khan, Muzafar-ud-daulah." Prominent among the mutinous officers was a Walloon called Liégeois—whether it was a real name or not, some of his descendants continued to bear it down to recent times under the slightly altered form of "Lezwah." This man, in constant communication with young Reinhardt, worked upon the simple minds of the soldiery till almost all were ready for any act of insubordination.[1]

The occasion was not to be long awaited. In 1794 Thomas had so far effected the conversion of the ill-advised Mewâtis as to extort from them an agreement to pay one year's land-revenue, besides obtaining possession of Tijara and Jhajar, two of their chief places. He was making preparation to attack the neighbouring fort of Bahadurgurh when he was suddenly recalled by the news that Levassoult was moving in his rear with the troops of his old employer, the Lady of Sardhana. Unwilling to risk a present and certain defeat if, with his ill-trained and raw levies, he encountered a large and

[1] Such names as Liégeois, Bernier, &c., would be surely mangled by the natives, according to their custom. A comrade of one of the Lezwahs was known to the present writer as Epiphan Shistan; but on the rolls of the office in which he served was entered as "Shaitân Ferryfund." At an earlier date Ochterlony was known as "Loni Attar" (Butter-and-meal).

well-disciplined force, Thomas fell back upon Tijara, leaving Levassoult to get what he could out of the unfortunate Mewâtis. In this place—Tijara—Thomas remained unmolested until summoned to the relief of his master, Appa Khandi Rao, who was in durance, in his camp, by reason of a mutiny. Hurrying to the spot, the faithful mercenary availed himself of the cover of a dark and rainy night to withdraw the Rao from a disagreeable and dangerous position, and Thomas escorted him to Kanaund, a strong place, already mentioned, of which we shall hear again later on.

For this piece of service the Rao showed a genuine, but not perhaps very expensive, form of gratitude, adopting Thomas as a son, and endowing him with valuable estates—belonging, doubtless, to other people but not the less generously offered. About the same time the agents of Sindhia at Dehli gave Thomas the first of several invitations to enter the Imperial service; invitations which the Irishman was always too independent to accept and of which the refusal ultimately caused his ruin.

Meanwhile Levassoult had made a direct attack upon Jhajar, named above as the second of the towns held by Thomas in the Mewâti country; but, while the latter was doing his best to meet the storm, it was rolled back by a sudden outburst elsewhere. Liégeois had at length succeeded in seducing from their allegiance the troops left in cantonments at Sardhana; and now Levassoult had to hurry home to protect his wife, who was threatened with violence there. In May, 1795, Liégeois repaired to Dehli, and there placed before Aloysius Reinhardt an agreement by which—with signs and crosses in lieu of signatures—his unlettered associates had bound themselves, in the name of the Holy Trinity, to do as Aloysius might command. As soon as the Begum and her husband had wind of what was doing, they appealed to the British Governor-General for advice and assistance, and received for answer permission to repair to Anupshahr, on the other side of the Duăb, and put themselves under the protection of Brigadier MacGowan.

In these anxieties the hot summer months passed, until the threatened couple had completed arrangements for escape from their perils. Having obtained the necessary authority from the Governor-General and from Sindhia, they departed from Sardhana in the dawn of an October morning, the Begum in her palanquin and Levassoult on horseback; they also carried with them portable property and specie which conduced to the frustration of the whole plan. Scarcely had they advanced three miles upon the way to Meerut when they saw dust-clouds rising behind them and guessed that their flight had been discovered and that they were followed by pursuers eager for the spoil. They therefore parted, with an agreement that if either should be slain, the other would not survive. Levassoult led the way, urging the groaning bearers of the treasure-chests to hurry on; but the pursuers came on fast; the litter was arrested; and the Begum, in sudden impulse, stabbed herself with a dagger. An attendant ran forward screaming and waving a bloodstained kerchief torn from the neck of her mistress, at sight of which Levassoult put a pistol to his head, drew the trigger, and fell lifeless from his saddle. The rebels turned back with the plunder, carrying the widowed Princess with them; her stiletto had not touched a vital part, and she soon recovered: but it was to find herself the prisoner of her abandoned stepson. Aloysius assumed the command, plunging forthwith into the frantic debauchery in which he and his ruffianly companions found their ideal of bliss; while the wounded Begum lay in the courtyard tied to a gun and only kept alive by the ministrations of a faithful Aya.

We have mentioned that a French officer named Saleur had been a friend of the deceased M. Levassoult and a witness of the too private marriage. This man, who had held aloof from the proceedings of his fellows, now bethought him of the ill-used Irishman; and, by a lucky chance, Thomas, in pursuit of his own plans, had moved his camp to no great distance. Saleur therefore sent him a report of what had happened, with a prayer for help. The gallant seaman, without a moment's delay, replied with a strong written remonstrance to his former comrades, pointing out that, if they persisted in their present conduct or presumed to injure the Begum, Sindhia would certainly disband the brigade and probably put them all to the sword. Swiftly following his message, he appeared at Sardhana, at the head of his *Khās Risāla*, or mounted bodyguard. The mutinous officers, ashamed of their late orgy and already weary of their new commander, alarmed by the reasonings of Thomas and swayed by a handsome douceur out of his generous munificence, returned to their allegiance. Aloysius was made prisoner and sent back to Dehli; and the restored Begum—though she never repaid the £20,000 which Thomas had expended on her liberation—never again gave way to the temptations of Hymen. Saleur in future commanded the brigade.

This romantic history rests on the evidence of James Skinner—of whom more anon—and exhibits our Tipperary mariner in a most favouring light, showing how gallant he was, how prompt and prodigal of purse and person. Meanwhile, Appa Khandi Rao had become hostile, whether from native fickleness or prompted by jealous rivals of the foreign employé; and the position of the latter might have become one of much anxiety had not his adoptive father suddenly lost his reason and committed suicide by drowning himself in the river Jumna.

Thomas at that moment was engaged in an expedition against the Sikhs, whom he ultimately drove beyond that river; and the power and property of the deceased Rao were, in his absence, assumed by the chief's nephew. It may be doubted how far the adoption of Thomas held good in Hindu law; in any case, he was either unwilling or unable to assert his claims.

But he was now becoming a man of mark. The Sikhs —who at that time were no more than a predatory horde of badly-horsed marauders—had had what Thomas called "a sample of my method of fighting"; and the Upper Duāb had been entirely delivered from their unwelcome presence. But he was now looking out for fresh employment, and accepted an engagement under Lakwa Dada, one of Sindhia's best Generals, to raise and train a considerable body of horse and foot in the frontier-district of Paniput, the scene of old campaigns. He got this second start in 1797, the beginning of a brief, but by no means inglorious, career.

It might, indeed, have ended in his entering the service of Sindhia permanently; but, as we have seen already, Thomas was wanting in worldly wisdom; and he preferred to run a solitary course, rather than plod on as a prosperous subordinate in a settled system.

Boigne might have conciliated the cometary man and brought him into a regular orbit; but that wise commander was now gone, and the reins had fallen into the hands of a far less competent successor, a Frenchman of low birth and breeding whose proper name was Pierre Cuiller, but who now assumed the style of "General Perron"; to whom a separate chapter will be devoted presently.

In the meanwhile we shall be content to bear in mind what has been said of the changed character of the French adventurers after the fall of the Bourbon monarchy. Up to that time the greater number had been cadets of good families seeking fortune by the aid of their swords; but now men of much humbler origin appeared in India, seeking a share of the good things understood to be at the disposal of the brave and skilful. Perron, as will be more fully shown hereafter, was singularly unlike Thomas in some important respects, although in his first introduction nearly his parallel, having deserted from before the mast of a vessel in Suffren's squadron about the same time that Thomas left the adverse fleet of Admiral Hughes. But the times were such that the most commonplace plebeian had scope for the loftiest ambition in Indian fields; and the dreams of Thomas were none the less likely to offend the views of Perron because of their romantic element. While Raymond was high in power at Haidarabad and Citizen Ripaud an ambassador between the Mauritius and Mysore, Perron may well have indulged in the framing of schemes in which he may have looked on the Irish seaman as a hostile element.

In the immediate present Thomas was giving but too much opening for criticism. When, in 1798, the Sikh danger had passed away, the Franco-Marathas at Dehli had no further use for him, and accordingly dispensed with his services. Consequently he and his followers had to adopt a predatory life on pain of starvation; and it is to be feared that he was now little better than a dacoit defying the police. His admirers may regret to have to say so, but the truth is paramount.

The fact is that Upper India was at this pass that every man was a law to himself. The landlords robbed the tenants, and the soldiers robbed the landlords; the only wonder is that there was anything left for any one. "It is a matter of fact," so an official record assures us, "that in those days the highways were unoccupied and travellers walked through byways. The facility of escape, the protection afforded by the heavy jungles, and the numerous forts that then studded the country, with the ready sale for plundered property, all combined to foster spoliation."[1] If this was the state of

[1] *Aligurh Statistics*, by Sherer and Hutchinson, Roorkee, 1856.

things at Aligurh, where Perron had his headquarters with all the best troops of the Government at his disposal, what must have been the condition of the tracts between Dehli and the desert, where Thomas was now operating?

Returning to Jhajar, the chivalrous buccaneer soon broke new ground by leading his men into the territory of the Jaipur State, which lay on the south of his present barren country. Sitting down before a small place not far from Kanaund, he demanded a ransom of one lakh, but accepted half of that sum on the fort capitulating under threat of assault. In the course of these transactions an unfortunate accident set fire to the town, and all was lost. After some further depredations in Jaipur lands, Thomas returned to his headquarters and began seriously to consider his future prospects.

It is probable that the district of Jhajar had not at times in itself the means of subsistence for even such a small body of men as he now commanded, during the time that must elapse before new engagements could be obtained. Sindhia's French officers, too, were not masters to his mind. Northern Jaipur had been ravaged; very possibly the forces of the State had taken possession of the wasted province; what was to be done?

The question was to be solved by the law of least resistance. On the southern side prudential considerations barred the way; on the east the Dehli territory was under the direct sway of the French; on the west lay the arid solitudes of Bikanir. But to the north was a tract of over three thousand square miles, known as Hariana ("Green-Land"), which was compact, capable, and without an owner. It contained many villages and small towns, with at least two more considerable places, both fortified; an ancient canal passed through, and to the north-west ran the river Caggar, leaving a deposit of fertilising silt after each rainy season. But the soil was stiff, so as to depend upon irrigation for its fertility;

and irrigation demanded constant labour, which had been rendered somewhat scarce by the ravages of a terrible famine that had depopulated the country in 1783–84.[1] Nevertheless the pasturage was generally good, the cattle were famous for strength and quality, the people were hardy, though somewhat lawless by reason of pastoral habits and long anarchy. In the midst of the district lay the two cities—Hánsi and Hisar—the latter being built on high ground and easily defensible. The failure of the water supply had acted disastrously on these places; the fort of each was in ruins, and the streets were filled with squalid houses and clay huts.

[1] Some details of this visitation have been recorded by the present writer in a former work (*Fall of the Moghal Empire*, 3rd ed., pp. 146, 147.) It was known, then and long after, as the *Chalisa Kant*,

CHAPTER IX

Thomas as the Raja of Hariana—His campaign in the Jaipur country—Dictator in Cis-Sutlej—Loyalty to British Crown—Perron's hostility, negotiations, and attack—Fall, captivity, and death of George Thomas.

THOMAS now underwent a wholesome change of view and conduct. About 1797 he had established himself at Hánsi. Here, as he told Colonel Francklin, his biographer, was his capital, where he rebuilt the decayed city walls and strengthened the defences of the fort. "As it (the town) had been long deserted, at first I found difficulty in providing inhabitants; but by degrees I selected between five and six thousand persons to whom I allowed every lawful indulgence. I established a mint and coined my own rupees, which I made current in my army and country,[1] as from the commencement of my career at Jhajar I had resolved to establish an independency. I employed workmen and artificers of all kinds, . . . cast my own artillery, commenced making muskets, matchlocks, and powder; and, in short, made the best preparations for carrying on a defensive and offensive war."

This lucid explanation is enough to show that the Irish tar's occasional deviations into a predatory life

[1] The present writer has met with one of these rupees. It is a small, thick coin, bearing the title of the Emperor Shah Alam in Persian, with a capital T in English character. He also conversed with one of Thomas's native officers at Hánsi in 1853, who spoke of the drinking-bouts of his old commander, but otherwise with admiration. Thomas was familiarly called "Sahib Bahadur."

From the Frontispiece of the "Life" by Francklin.

were no more than a small part of his permanent programme, and we must now consider the whilom free-lance in the position of an independent potentate. For a brief moment he had realised a mighty dream.

His prudence was not always active; but at this moment it was reconcilable with his ambition. The field in Hindustan being occupied by stronger powers, the Sailor-Raja naturally looked in the direction of the Punjab. "I wished," he said afterwards, "to put myself in a capacity of attempting the conquest of the Punjab, and aspired to the honour of planting the British standard on the banks of the Attock." This might have been done then, perhaps, had Thomas been left alone; but there was a young man growing up among the Sikhs whose efforts were to make the task another matter when it came to be done, half a century later.[1]

Another mark of superior judgment which our adventurer showed at this period was his care for his men, whom he not only paid well, but encouraged by providing a pension-fund for the benefit of their families. Rs. 40,000 were to be set aside for this purpose yearly; and as long as his powers lasted the pensions were punctually paid. At the same time he strenuously bore down all opposition to his authority, which by the first month of 1799 had been firmly consolidated in the greater part of the province. He had, indeed, now a real and respectable power. Besides his older acquisitions to the southward—of which the revenues sufficed for the maintenance of his army and the connected arsenals, he derived from his new lands the net income of two hundred and fifty estates (formerly rated at about £170,000 sterling a year) which he hoped to raise to their old prosperity. His military force was not, at this time, very large; he had, however, three well-drilled

[1] This, of course, was Ranjit Singh, of the Shukarcharia clan, born at Gujranwala about 1780, and now chieftain by the recent death of his father (*v. Ranjit Singh*, by Sir Lepel Griffin, "Rulers of India," Oxford, 1894).

battalions under British or Indo-British commanders, with fourteen guns, and his *Khās Risāla* of Pathan cavalry. With this contingent he presently took the field in a new attack upon the Jaipur State, by the invitation of his old master's nephew—the Maratha Wital Rao—acting, however, not as a subordinate, but as an independent ally, and stipulating for compensation in specie. After some temporary successes the invaders learned that the Raja was marching against them in person, at the head of 40,000 Rājputs inured to battle. The Maratha pronounced for an immediate retreat, but Thomas persuaded him to remain; and they took possession of the walled town of Fatehpur, on the north-west of the State, in the sandy neighbourhood of the great desert. No trees were to be seen save the thorny acacia known in those regions as *Babool*, but of this Thomas found enough, when cut down and shaped, to make an *abattis* in front of the town, by the wall of which his rear was sufficiently protected.

Hardly had he completed his works when the hostile columns began to appear. The adventurer was now in a grave position, confronted by an overwhelming force, supported by an ally of proved incompetence, and dependent for deliverance on his own skill and the courage of a comparatively small force of mercenaries. On the third day after their arrival the enemy made a formal commencement of the leaguer, on which Thomas resolved on an offensive defence, making a sortie against a body of 7,000 Rājputs who had advanced to cut off his water supply by seizing on the neighbouring wells. Taking two battalions and eight field-pieces, escorted by a few troopers, Thomas repulsed the Rājputs; but next morning was set upon by the main body of their army. His Maratha allies proved useless; but the result of his unaided efforts is a lesson to all good soldiers, not, indeed, to despise any enemy, but neither to despair because they are outnumbered.

The foe advanced in three divisions: one to threaten the camp, a second to occupy the town, the third to try conclusions with the followers of the audacious white man. This last force might well appear to menace destruction to the isolated invaders, being composed of no less than ten regular battalions, with the marksmen of the Raja's bodyguard, a quantity of cavalry, and twenty-two guns. The General-in-Chief led them on against Thomas and his two thousand, who took post on a sand-hill to await the attack while their comrades defended the town. In the end Thomas not only repulsed the attack, but was able to hasten to the aid of the garrison, while that small but well-commanded force, observing his approach, came out in rear of the enemy, who were thus placed between two fires. Thrown into confusion and having no good leaders, the vast multitude broke and scattered in flight. Some time was now lost in persuading the Maratha horse to take up the pursuit, and Thomas admits the loss of two twenty-four pounders which—according to his narrative—remained embedded in the sand. He adds that he lost 300 of his men and a European officer; and he had ultimately to retire from the invaded territory along with his pusillanimous ally.

This strange account rests on the unsupported evidence of George Thomas; but, seeing that his narrative is always confirmed by independent testimony in all cases where such is forthcoming, it may be received with some confidence here. Certain it is that he was not hindered in retiring with the bulk of his force, and that neither then nor on any subsequent occasion did the Raja of Jaipur ever venture on attacking him; while Thomas had sustained so little damage that, before the summer was over, he had made another raid into the western sands, and harried the possessions of the Raja of Bikanir, who had co-operated with his brother of Jaipur during the late campaign. From him Thomas extorted a handsome indemnity, and next turned his attention to his former enemies, the Cis-Sutlej Sikhs.

While thus employed he received an invitation from Ambaji, one of Sindhia's generals, to join in an expedition against Udaipur. His share in this brief campaign was probably of little importance; but the period is so far noticeable that it showed the beginnings of unruliness among the troops, and of hostility on the part of General Perron. Against his own men Thomas displayed a resolute firmness; and, when ordered, in the name of Sindhia, to separate from Ambaji, he replied that he was acting under that General and could take orders from no one else.

At the end of 1799 Thomas was once more back at Hánsi; but before the end of the cold weather set off to renew his campaign against the Sikhs of Jhind and Patiala. In this, as he reports, "I had been more successful than I could possibly expect when I took the field with a force of 5,000 men and thirty-six pieces of cannon. I lost, in killed, wounded, and disabled, nearly one-third of my men, but the enemy lost 5,000. I realised nearly two lakhs (say £20,000), and was to receive an additional lakh for the hostages."

Thomas was now at his zenith, "Dictator," as he said, "in all the countries south of the Sutlej." Had his prudence and his diplomatic ability equalled his other gifts, he might have altered the history of Hindustan. As often happens, he was his own worst enemy, offending his neighbours by reckless raiding, utterly defying authority, when exercised by a Frenchman, and (occasionally at least) immoderate in the use of intoxicating liquor. That he, about this time, threw away good cards is very plain. At the beginning of the year 1800, the last French danger to the British Government on the southern side of India had been removed by the fall of "Citizen Tippu"; while in Hindustan Daulat Rao Sindhia was looking askance at General Perron, and divided between hatred of the English and fear of Jaswant Rao Holkar, who was adopting a very threatening attitude. In this conjuncture Thomas opened negotiations with Holkar and with Begum Sombre, at the same time employing the friendly intervention of Captain E. V. White, with a view to obtain the support of Lord Wellesley in Calcutta.

George, who had left Ireland many years before 1798, was always a loyal British subject. He now proposed to occupy the Punjab and place his conquests at the disposal of the Government. "I have nothing in view," he said, "but the welfare of my country and King. I shall be sorry to see my conquests fall to the Marathas; I wish to give them to my King." Certain necessary conditions being assumed, there was nothing unreasonable in the aspiration. The Sikhs, as has been shown, were not then the formidable opponents they were to become under Ranjit Singh, with a new generation of foreign officers, and Thomas easily beat them whenever he wished. In the opinion of Major L. F. Smith (a writer to whom we are constantly driven in studying the time) the substitution of Thomas for Perron at the head of Sindhia's Regulars needed little more than a word from Wellesley; and Smith further assures us that the officers of British birth, of whom he was one, would have rallied round Thomas whatever the French might do. But it would seem that the importance of all this was not known to the Calcutta authorities; or, perhaps, the Peace of Amiens was already dawning on the vision of far-seeing statesmen. Wellesley was in somewhat intimate correspondence with the Prime Minister, and knew that First Consul Bonaparte had reasons for desiring to be on good terms with our nation. About this time the Consul wrote, with this design, his famous letter to George III.; and, though duly snubbed by the Cabinet of St. James's, he was only waiting for events which ere long opened the way to a treaty. In these circumstances the

Governor-General may well have refrained from interference with French influence in Upper India. The abstinence proved a mistake; British interference, postponed for a couple of years, found the Marathas in greater strength and union, the friendly Sailor-Raja of Hariana being no longer there to help.

These matters will be dealt with more appropriately in the account of General Perron. Here we have only to notice their effect on the waning strength of George Thomas. Early in 1801 he nerved himself for a final effort, augmenting his little army and leading the best and largest portion to a fresh foray against the Sikhs, in the course of which he got within four marches of Lahore. Here he received intelligence that Perron had conducted a raid into Hariana—instigated, it is thought, by an appeal for aid from the Punjab. With habitual decision Thomas at once set his face homewards: beating off the Sikh horse who tried to harass his retreat, and rushing his men along at the rate of from thirty to forty miles a day, he reached Hánsi, only to find the birds of prey flown. Perron, discovering that he had made a mistake in attacking Thomas with so small a force, retired rapidly to Dehli; but he presently returned with reinforcements. In August, 1801, the two armies drew near to each other at Bahadurgurh, about fifteen miles west of Dehli.

Perron, with or without an honest desire for peace, invited negotiation, and Major L. F. Smith was sent to the Hánsi camp to invite George to discuss preliminaries in a personal interview with the French General. With our knowledge of the warm patriotism of the one, and the almost certain ambition of the other, we are prepared for a failure. "Mr. Perron and himself," Thomas afterwards said, "being subjects of two nations then in a state of hostility, it was impossible that they should act in concert; . . . he was moreover convinced that, as a Frenchman, Mr. Perron would always be prepared to misrepresent his actions." He was willing, he added, to take part in the conduct of operations anywhere; but he informed Sindhia that he could act only under an Asiatic General. When at length persuaded to go to Perron's camp, he took an escort of his best men, and went, as he said, "prepared to observe the greatest circumspection in the interview."

A discussion conducted in this spirit was not likely to end well. Perron stated his ultimatum with due plain-speaking. Thomas was required to surrender the lands of Jhajar, to enter the service on a fixed monthly salary, and to detach immediately four battalions to assist Sindhia against Holkar, who had just driven the army of Sindhia before him and taken his city of Ujain. The spirit of Thomas would not brook these terms, specious as they appeared; he was in friendly communication with Holkar; he suspected Sindhia of treachery; he was determined not to serve under Perron. He accordingly, to use his own language, "without further discussion, abruptly broke up the conference and marched away in disgust." He retired to Hánsi, while Perron went back to his own head-quarters at Aligurh, leaving the campaign to be conducted by an officer of his own nation, Major Louis Bernard Bourquin. Thomas had thrown a garrison into his fort of Georgegurh, commanded by a native officer named Shatab Khan; and Perron was able to put pressure on this person by reason of his being an Aligurh man, the members of whose family were at Perron's disposal. Another diplomatic move was made by inciting the Sikhs to invade the north of the district; Begum Sombre, too, was called upon for a contingent, which she sent; and reinforcements were ordered up from Agra. Surrounded by this ring of fire, our poor adventurer was brought to bay; he sent an earnest appeal to Holkar, and, without waiting for a reply, betook himself to the north, as if to encounter the Sikhs, but in reality hoping to draw off the attention of the invaders from Hánsi, where he had his stores and where his family were residing. In this move he was successful; Smith's brother being left with a detachment to watch Georgegurh, the bulk of the army marched towards Jhind in pursuit of Thomas. That adventurer now doubled back unperceived by the enemy, reached Georgegurh by marching seventy miles in two days, and put Smith to flight with a loss of 700 men, besides arms, baggage, and ammunition. This was about the 26th of September; next day Bourquin's cavalry reached Biri, a village near Georgegurh, and at once made a reconnaissance of Thomas's camp. They found it skilfully pitched, with a village on the left, the fort on the right, and the front defended by a line of sand heaps, probably artificial. The rear was also partly protected by another village.

On the afternoon of the 29th, Bourquin came up, and, without affording the men time to rest, immediately ordered an attack, supported by the fire of thirty-five guns. But the shot fell into the sand; the wearied infantry could do little; twenty-five of Bourquin's tumbrils were exploded by shot from the enemy's batteries. Then two battalions sallied from the works under an officer named Hopkins, who "delivered a volley as if they had been at a review," and charged Bourquin's left with such vigour that it gave way in complete confusion. Night separated the combatants; in the morning a truce was made, and it appeared that out of 8,000 men the assailants had lost one half in killed and wounded, amongst them being four European officers, one of whom was the younger Smith, who was shot dead. Thomas had lost only 700 men, but amongst them was Captain Hopkins, whose leg had been broken by a round shot during the last charge, and who died of his hurt a few days later. Hopkins was the son of a British officer who had left him to make his way in the world, encumbered with the charge of an unmarried sister, and Thomas in this hour of his own distress found means to send Miss Hopkins Rs. 2,000 for her present necessities, with a promise of more should more be required.

But he was himself now almost at his last resources. Shatab Khan, the commandant of the fort, treacherously fired all the fodder; and Thomas, apparently losing his wonted energy, remained inactive for a month, hoping, perhaps, that help might come from Holkar.[1] Finally, finding himself deserted, with neither forage for the cattle nor food for the men, with treachery undermining his resources and his men deserting daily, Thomas conceived the enterprise of cutting his way through the investing enemies and throwing himself into Hánsi, there to make a final stand.

Accordingly, at nine o'clock on the evening of the 10th November, accompanied by his two remaining Christian officers, Hearsey and Birch, escorted by his bodyguard and mounted on a fine Persian horse, Thomas burst out, drove off a party of the enemy who tried to intercept him, and, making a considerable circuit, reached Hánsi next day. It is pleasant to know that the animal who carried his master a hundred and twenty miles in twenty-four hours was nobly provided for, and long survived in the stable of Sir F. Hamilton, Bart., the British resident at Benares. The soldiers left in camp laid down their arms with loud lamentations; and, refusing to serve another leader, departed for their own homes by permission of the victors.

Arrived at his capital, Thomas prepared for its defence, casting guns and strengthening the fortifications. On the 21st November the besiegers opened their trenches, and, after some sorties, effected an entry within the walls, though the citadel still held out. Thomas had still his

[1] Skinner thought that Thomas had a long bout of drink and consequent incapacity at this period.

two faithful friends and about 1,700 men, and with these he continued his resistance. In these operations the leader of the Begum's contingent was killed.[1] At daybreak on the 3rd December three strong columns advanced to the assault, and Thomas came out to meet them, clothed in chain armour like a Crusader of old. The enemy, as we are informed by James Skinner, who was among them, lost 1,600 men; and he adds, "We had to come several times to hand-to-hand fighting." Skinner's brother attacked Thomas sword in hand, but could make no impression on his coat-of-mail. The Homeric conflict was renewed next morning, and trenches were traced within two hundred yards of the fort; but all in vain: the cannon buried harmless shot in the earthen ramparts, and the fearless George, roused from his drunkenness, drove off the assailants with the old cheerful daring. Recourse was now had to mining, and Bourquin openly boasted that he was suborning the soldiers of the garrison, and was determined to take Thomas alive or dead.

All the gallantry of the Irishman was ultimately to no purpose. He had stood against enormous odds for three months, defying the power that was paramount in Hindustan; and, after such exertions, and inflicting on the enemy a loss of so many thousands of brave men, he was more outmatched than ever. Revenge must be had for this, thought Bourquin, with the ferocity of a low and selfish nature. Moreover, the desperate defence of an untenable position is an offence against the laws of war, and Bourquin had cause for anger without the generosity of nature which would mitigate such feeling in a better man. He openly boasted to his officers of the terrible example that he would make of Thomas. The conversation occurred at tiffin in the mess-tent,

[1] This was Captain Bernier, mentioned above as one of the witnesses of the Begum's marriage with Levassoult. Skinner calls him "Mr. Bunnear."

and the Europeans and East Indians present were shocked at the Frenchman's cruelty of purpose. The meal being over and the *mollia tempora fandi* coming on, these worthy fellows united in respectful but firm remonstrance, to which Bourquin so far yielded as to consent to an attempt being made to get Thomas to yield without delay or further fighting. Despite the loss of his brother, Major Smith undertook the task, and repaired to the fort under a flag of truce. The forlorn adventurer was open to reason, as his friendly visitor pointed out to him the cruelty of demanding further sacrifices from his followers in pursuing what was so easily seen to be a vain resistance. "Considering," said Thomas, "that I had entirely lost my party, and with it the hope of *at present* subduing the Sikhs and powers in the French interest; that I had no expectation of succour from any quarter . . . in this situation I agreed to evacuate the fort."

He surrendered on the first day of the year 1802, being allowed to retain his arms, his family, and his private property, consisting of three lakhs of rupees in specie, shawls, and jewellery. Honourable terms were also given to the garrison. What was to be the next phase was still unsettled, when Thomas decided the question by an outbreak which did not admit of any hope of permanent relations. The officers had made him an honorary member of their mess, where he indulged freely in those habits of conviviality for which he was always known. One evening, after the cloth had been removed, the talk turned on politics. The Peace of Amiens was not yet concluded, and Perron was engaging—as we shall see presently—in schemes for opposing the English in Hindustan. "Well!" cried Bourquin, lifting his glass, "here's success to General Perron!" Most of the guests ignored the invitation; but that was not enough for the Irishman, who considered it a deliberate insult. Drawing his sword, he rushed at Bourquin, who had only time to escape from the mess-tent and hide himself in that devoted to the zenana. Thomas, in his elation, sprang upon the table, where he stood waving his sword and calling on all, with peals of hoarse laughter, to bear witness that he made "the Frenchman run like a jackal."[1] Being presently pacified, he allowed himself to be conducted to his quarters. On arriving at the fort they found a sentry standing at the gate, and were—as a matter of course—challenged with "Who goes there?" "Sahib Bahadur," answered Thomas, giving the name he was wont to give to his own men on such occasions. On the sentinel answering that this was not the watch-word, the fallen hero's passion returned. "Not know Sahib Bahadur?" he cried, and cut the poor fellow down. It was necessary to get rid of such a guest, and the next day Thomas, with his family and his goods, was escorted to Sardhana by the still friendly Smith.

Thomas had married a French dependent of the Begum's whose Christian name was Marie, and she had borne him three sons and a daughter. These—mother and children—he left in charge of the Begum, with a lakh of rupees for their support. The Begum, it should be remembered, was deeply indebted to him, for money and for yet more; she accepted the charge and acquitted herself fairly well. An oil-painting of one of the sons—John—which used to hang in the palace at Sardhana, is evidence that the subject was a man of some considera-tion; his dress is handsome, though it is in the Asiatic style. The daughter is believed to have been married at Dehli and to have left issue there; and the grand-daughter of another son, James, was living at Agra a few years back, the wife of a Mr. Martin. A third son was in the service of Ranjit Singh, and rose to the command of a regiment.

Thomas went on to Anupshahr, whence he was, by order of the British Government, put on board a boat

[1] The words are recorded by Skinner, who was present.

accompanied by Captain Francklin[1]—afterwards known as the author of several works on Indian history. As they floated slowly down the river, Thomas dictated to Francklin a quantity of information about the Sikhs and other tribes among or against whom he had been engaged; and—what is perhaps more generally interesting now—gave him an account of his life to which we have been indebted for most of our present record. But the change of life was too much for the adventurer's constitution, tried as it had been; and he died at Bahrampur on the 22nd of August, being—as was supposed—in his 46th year.

That George Thomas was the equal of General de Boigne is not to be maintained, the latter having been a military officer of good education, while poor George was but a Tipperary bog-trotter, trained on board a man-of-war such as is described by Smollett. To have risen in a few years from the forecastle to be the leader of an army and the ruler of a State, must needs have demanded no common gifts and exertions; and we may perhaps see in this forgotten wanderer more than the germs of a true hero. He was tall and handsome, a master of the Hindustani idiom, and able to read and write Persian; and, what is much more, he was true, generous, and brave, and a patriotic subject of that Empire of which his native island was, is, and must be, a most important part.

[1] Francklin, Captain G., *Military Memoir of G. Thomas*, 4to. Calcutta, 1803. There is a similar book on Jas. Skinner by Baillie Fraser (London, 1851). Both are in the India Office.

CHAPTER X

Condition of the Begum's Sirdhana principality not good, or only good as compared with other districts—Ill-fortune of J. H. Bellasis—The Hessings, father and son—Fate of some of Holkar's Christian officers—French under Perron.

ALTHOUGH the Begum Sombre was not strictly a "European adventurer," the remainder of her story may be worth a brief notice for the light that it throws on the condition of the part of the country where her fief lay, and on the nature of the steps by which it was gradually delivered from anarchy. By the time of the flying visit paid by Thomas at Sardhana, the Begum's affairs had become finally settled; and she had no more serious troubles to the day of her death, nearly forty years later. The worst of Sombre's followers were dead, dismissed, or subdued. M. Saleur was in command; Bernier, his Lieutenant, had been killed, leading the contingent against Hánsi, as mentioned in the preceding chapter. Stepson Aloysius had died in 1801, and his tomb is still to be seen in the desecrated church at Agra; he left a daughter, married in due time to a Mr. Dyce, a somewhat dour Scotchman, who was bailiff of the landed estates. These were managed on a hard but efficient system under which the tillers of predial land were little better than predial serfs, from whom the management endeavoured to recover the whole of the net produce. Nevertheless, the little principality, with outlying dependencies beyond the river Jumna, was a real oasis of plenty among the war-worn tracts by which it was surrounded; and the fear of falling from bad to worse kept the peasantry from their natural means of defence—escape to other lands. Contemporary history shows that the dread of losing labourers was, in those evil days, the only check upon rapine and misrule. "The sword rose, the hind fell"; the field turned to forest; and the miserable husbandmen flocked to the Begum's territory as to a land of milk and honey. In 1840, when the Princess was dead, the Revenue Board at Agra sent an officer to make the necessary fiscal arrangements; and this gentleman reported that in those favoured regions the rates of assessment on the cultivation averaged about one-third higher than what prevailed in the adjoining territory under British rule. Now the British demand of those days professed to be two-thirds of the net rental; what, then, could have been left to the Begum's tenants? As the British territory had been at peace for more than a generation, the Begum had not latterly enjoyed her old advantages; and an observer of a few years earlier noted that, under her administration, cultivators were compelled to till the land by the presence of soldiers with fixed bayonets; luckily there were no native newspapers! The first act of the Board, after receiving the report of the settlement-officer, was at once to reduce the total assessment of the province from nearly *seven lakhs* (Rs. 691,388) to a little over *five*. Further, a whole schedule of miscellanies was abolished, including export and import dues, taxes on "animals; wearing apparel, cloth of every description; sugar-cane, spices, and all other produce, . . . transfer of lands and houses and sugar-works, . . . the latter very high." The result of all this had been that, for the last few years, many of the estates had been deserted and thrown on the hands of the management, who made the best they could out of them by means of hired labour. The population rapidly returned under the new *régime* (*Reports of Revenue Settlement*, N.-W.P., vol. i.).[1]

[1] For a few further particulars regarding Sardhana, see Appendix.

Meanwhile our modern Deborah judged her people and increased her store. When, in 1803, Generals Arthur Wellesley and Stevenson marched into the Deccan, Sindhia was assisted by the Begum's contingent under Saleur, and they formed the guard of camp and baggage during the sanguinary struggle of Asai. On the 1st of November Lake overcame the forces of Ambaji at Laswări, and the Begum had to mend her ways. Seated once more in the historic palanquin in which she had already seen and suffered, she was borne into the camp of the Commander-in-Chief, arriving in the evening just as dinner was over. On the announcement of her arrival Lake rose hastily and went to the door of his tent in time to catch her Highness in the act of descending from the litter. In the excitement of the moment the General gave his visitor a hearty kiss: "See, my friends!" cried the self-possessed lady to her attendants, "how the Padre receives his penitent child." The red coat and face of this jolly father of the Church militant are said to have struck the bystanders with astonishment; but the result was a complete success. The Begum was confirmed in a life-tenure of all her possessions, Lake having plenary political authority from the Calcutta Government; and for the rest of her days she maintained a sort of mediatised rule in her provincial capital. Of her palace and church—still standing—as of the unhappy offspring of the harsh land-agent and the grand-daughter of Sombre who became the Begum's heir, of all the litigation that followed, this is hardly the place to speak. Our business is with the state of Hindustan before the British occupation; and those who desire an entertaining summary of this later history of Sardhana may be referred to the *Gentleman's Magazine*, vol. 280, pp. 459, ff.

Hitherto we have been dealing with cases of persons more or less known by name; but many of the adventurers, especially towards the end, when they

PALACE AT SARDHANA.

From a Sketch by the Author.

became numerous, have been seldom heard of beyond the circle of their own families and by the few who have had the opportunity of coming across the record of Louis Ferdinand Smith. Of such was a gifted but unfortunate gentleman, Joseph Harvey Bellasis.

Bellasis was an English gentleman who began life as an officer in the Bengal Engineers. About the year 1796—the period of the mutiny against Sir John Shore—there was great and general discontent among the officers of the Bengal Army; and Bellasis, with others, saw fit to leave the service. Being yet young, he sought for fortune in the employ of one of the quarrelsome "native Powers" who were then contesting the miserable remains of the once mighty Moghal Empire. He had seen instances of men, with advantages inferior to his own, rising to place and wealth in such employment; and he willingly engaged in the army of Daulat Rao Sindhia, under the immediate command of Ambaji Ainglia, often mentioned in these pages. He is reported by Smith to have possessed all the gifts of "undaunted courage, an excellent education, an elegant person, great activity of body and energy of mind; he was generous, open, candid, and affable, an accomplished scholar and finished gentleman, of fascinating address."

How all these talents failed to command success the remainder of the short story will show, though without fully disclosing the reasons of failure. Ambaji was, perhaps, an unfortunate selection in the first introduction of a high-class Englishman entering the native service, being always noted for his opposition to the British interest and for his leanings towards Jaswant Rao Holkar, who was the rival of his master, Sindhia; he was also a man of parsimonious habit, and—apparently—of restless and imprudent nature. At the beginning of their relations he was favourable to the new recruit, whom he commissioned to raise four battalions. These, according to Smith, would have made the finest body of its size in Hindustan, if only Ambaji had provided properly for their equipment and pay. Bellasis felt indignation at his chief's parsimony, which he did not attempt to conceal; apparently his character was deficient in the suppleness which must have been requisite in a foreigner anxious to win his way with an Asiatic master. A little later—about three years before the end of the century—another Maratha General, Lakwa Dada, was engaging himself in the cause of the "Bais," widows of the great Mahadaji (whom the new Sindhia was ungratefully plundering and persecuting), and was suddenly dismissed from the service and driven into active revolt. All Central India was instantly in commotion, the rebel chief occupying several places of strength between Bundelkhand and the Gwalior territory, in alliance with the Raja of Dattia, a petty State bordering on Jhansi. Ambaji proceeded to attack the confederates with several brigades of regular troops, that newly raised by Bellasis being one. The latter was presently ordered to capture Lahar, a very strong position about midway between Gwalior and Kalpi; and he performed the service—which was full of risk and difficulty—as well as if he had been leading the best troops in the world rather than a raw levy. But he met with an ungenerous return: the assault of Lahar had severely tried his men, and before they had rested, or even buried their dead, Bellasis was bid to march them off to the storm of another fortress. Then he lost patience, and addressed a strong remonstrance to the Maratha General, pointing out that his compliance with the order would leave him without the means of providing for the care of his wounded, while there was no urgent necessity such as might demand the sacrifice. The enraged barbarian expelled him from the camp and confiscated his property. The young officer was now sorely tried: he had lost his position in the British army, and found himself stranded in a foreign land without the means of subsistence. In this extremity Bellasis had to swallow his pride and sue for reinstalment; as he was a useful, however touchy, servant, his prayer was granted; and he was presently employed in a new campaign in the same part of the country. This was a war which Daulat Rao had begun against his own overlord, the Peshwa or President of the Maratha confederacy. In December, 1799, it fell to the lot of Bellasis to lead another forlorn hope; Perron had now repaired to the scene of war, and found it necessary to assault a place called Saunda, in the Dattia State; Bellasis headed the stormers with his wonted valour, and was shot through the head while mounting the breach. "Thus," writes the chronicler, "fell poor Bellasis, an ornament to society and an honour to his nation, . . . whose heart was pure and unsullied, and his sentiments noble and refined."

A very different destiny awaited men of far less merit. Two of the later Brigadiers of Sindhia's regulars were John Hessing and Brownrigg; of the latter we need only note that, like Skinner, Shepherd, Gardner, and Sutherland, he refused to join Perron against the British, and all were ultimately provided with posts or pensions from the Company. The short career of the Hessings—father and son—demands a more detailed notice.

Hessing was a native of the Netherlands who had served in the army of the first Sindhia ever since it was reorganised in 1789: he is described by Smith as "a good, benevolent man and a brave officer." This guarded estimate accords with the facts of the case. In 1790—about the time of the campaign against Ismail Khan, and when Hessing could not have been many months in the service, he incurred Boigne's displeasure to such a degree that he was obliged to leave his battalion. Sindhia, however, took compassion on him and gave him the command of the *Khās Risāla*—his personal troop or bodyguard—on his last visit to Poona in the early part of the year 1792. Hessing, however, does not seem to have remained long there; for, about the time of

Sindhia's death in 1794, he had made over the body-guard to his son and gone to Agra, where he was put in charge of the fort. But in 1801, when the force had been augmented, the son took part in the important campaign against Holkar, the fortunes of which vacillated so remarkably in Malwa. Perron, for some reason, did not take the command on this occasion ; perhaps did not like to be far away while Thomas was being hunted down. Old Hessing, indeed, never returned to active service, and soon after died in his bed at Agra. So the common-place Dutchman, who had actually lived, in that stormy time, the life of the fabled halcyon, died before the evil days came ; and while the bones of the brilliant Bellasis lay in an unmarked ditch of Bundelkhand, his remains were interred in the finest monument of the whole cemetery, fashioned in the likeness of the famous Taj Mahal and decorated by a fulsome epitaph as long as a leading article in a newspaper. Such are the ironies of Fate.

The younger Hessing was a man of crude tactics and doubtful military merit. At a great battle under the walls of Ujain, Holkar broke his line with cavalry charges, and killed or wounded—mainly killed—four-fifths of the force. Of the European officers, Captains Graham, Urquhart, and Macpherson, with four sub-alterns, were all slain in defending the guns ; Major Deridon, Captain Duprat, and Lieutenant Humpherstone were made prisoners ; Hessing owed his safety to the speed of his horse. His next appearance was in 1803, after the death of his father ; he raised the 5th Brigade at Agra, and was in charge of his father's old post, the command of the fort. When Lake arrived in October, Hessing, Sutherland, and five other European officers were put in arrest by the men, who feared their complicity with the British, but had to ask their intervention a few days later when they perceived the impossibility of making any further defence. By the mediation of these gentlemen terms were obtained from Lake, and they were provided for at the peace which shortly ensued. Of young Hessing no further record is requisite. Sutherland died some years later, and was buried at Mathra—where his tomb is to be seen still; Deridon founded a family of farmers, whose present representatives have preserved few signs of their European origin; Brownrigg, a gallant young fellow of approved and exceptional merit, was employed by the British Government, and finally killed in action at Sirsa, fighting the lawless Bhatti population, who had been only partially tamed by Thomas.

Just at the end of its existence the trained force underwent some serious trials. The war against the Dattia Raja, in whose country Bellasis lost his life, does not seem to have proved deadly to any other of the adventurers. On the 5th of January, 1800, after Perron had gone to the theatre of operations and assumed the command, a severe action took place, in which the chief command, under Perron, was held by James Shepherd, to whom Ambaji had given the charge of five battalions. The action was undecisive, and it was not until May 3rd that the overthrow of the confederates could be completed. On that day the infantry on their side was led by an Irish officer named William Henry Tone, brother to the well-known Theobald Wolfe Tone, and himself a man of character and acquirements. Poor old Lakwa Dada was at last driven from the field, and shortly after died of disappointment and fatigue at a sacred shrine where he had taken sanctuary. The Dattia Raja was killed fighting, and Colonel Tone—though he got off on that occasion—met a soldier's death next year, in the employ of Holkar. Colonel Shepherd soon after joined the British, and was given service in the Bundelkhand Police.

Of others of Holkar's officers a more tragic record

than that of Tone remains to be told. Jaswant Rao, though a gallant leader of horse, was a brutal enough barbarian by nature and made himself worse by habitual intemperance, which finally ruined his reason and abridged his days. On the Chevalier du Drenec leaving his service to join his French compatriots in the service of Sindhia, Holkar promoted an Anglo-Indian named Vickers to the command of the vacant brigade, two others being under the charge of two excellent officers, named Harding and Armstrong. On the 25th of October, 1802, after the failure of Thomas—with whom he would have been wiser to have co-operated—Holkar was brought to bay at Indore, Sindhia's army being commanded by Sutherland. The battle was fiercely fought. Mindful of the success of the year before at Ujain, Holkar made a vigorous charge of horse, covered by a general cannonade. The enemy's line was broken, but formed again under protection of a counter-charge by Sindhia's bodyguard. While the fight was thus swaying to and fro, in mediæval fashion, among the horsemen, Vickers advanced in line and routed six of Sindhia's battalions; but Captain Dawes opposed his further progress at the head of four of the old regiments, Boigne's veterans, whose backs no enemy had ever seen. Then Holkar brought up his cavalry once more and renewed the carnage. Dawes and two subalterns were slain, the European gunners were cut down in their batteries, where Holkar himself got two wounds, and Major Harding was killed at his side. Of the loss in rank and file there is no record.

It is sad to follow the fate of the gallant Vickers. After Lake's victories in 1803, Holkar felt that he might well be the next object of attack; and, indeed, he knew that he deserved it. One of his officers had the luck to be absent, as will appear later; but Colonel Vickers (with Major Dodd, Major Ryan, and four subalterns) was beheaded by the truculent chief on their boldly telling him that they could not bear arms against the British.

Of the brothers Smith a very few more words will be sufficient. The younger, as we saw, was killed at the beginning of the deplorable campaign of 1801, a campaign that need never have been fought but for the ambition of Perron and the too ardent patriotism of George Thomas. The elder was pensioned after the conquest of 1803-4, and appears to have settled in Calcutta, perhaps on the staff of the *Telegraph*, a paper published in that city, finally bringing out the little volume to which we have been so much indebted.

A few French and other Continental officers remain to be just named. Colonel Duprat commanded the 8th Brigade in 1798, his claim to promotion arising from a nefarious attempt to capture the Bais—widows of Mahadaji—from the camp of Amrit Rao, on the 7th June of the preceding year. Colonel Drugeon, however, was more successful in a later enterprise of the same sort, when Amrit, accepting Sindhia's assurances that molestation should cease, ventured to return to Poona (which he had left in not unnatural alarm). As the son of Raghunath Rao—whom the English called Ragoba—Amrit Rao should have known by experience both what Sindhia was and what was the general value of Maratha faith; yet he trusted; perhaps, however, he could not help himself. Drugeon watched his opportunity. One morning, on the last day of a great Muslim festival, he and his men came down to the river-side at Kirki—opposite to where Amrit was encamped with the ladies—affecting to be interested in the religious solemnities and the movements of the crowd. Suddenly, a screen of his men removing from the bank, the gallant Colonel opened fire on the defenceless ladies' tents from twenty-five field-pieces, and before the guard could rally from their first natural consternation, Drugeon was across the river and made prisoners the occupants of the tents.[1] In November of the following year the Colonel was put in charge of the palace and person of the blind Emperor at Dehli, Duprat succeeding to his brigade. In 1799 he was, for some unexplained reason, replaced by Sutherland, not usually a favourite with Perron, who—as will be observed more fully hereafter—seldom confided in a man of British blood. Perron soon afterwards removed Sutherland from this command, which he bestowed on Colonel Pohlmann, who was either an Alsatian or a German. Of this officer we only know further that he had a command in the Deccan when it was invaded by Stevenson and Arthur Wellesley; and, with the support of another brigade under Colonel Duprat, he made that stiff resistance at Asai that cost the future Duke of Wellington a full third of his army; one regiment (the 74th foot) lost no less than 17 officers, with 400 rank and file and non-commissioned; out of ten staff-officers only two escaped, and the young General's horse was shot dead under him, while his orderly trooper was killed at his side. What became of Pohlmann eventually is not recorded; most of the French officers are supposed to have returned to Europe, but Pohlmann and Shepherd appear to have taken service under the East India Company.

[1] See Grant Duff's *History of the Mahrattas*, ii. 320.

COLONEL G. W. HESSING.

GENERAL PERRON.

COLONEL ROBERT SUTHERLAND.

From Miniatures in the possession of S. Sutherland, Esq.

CHAPTER XI

Rise of Perron—Is employed against Ismail Beg—Perron's great prosperity—Character of civil administration.

THE chief interest of the concluding portion of the story arises out of the character and conduct of the officer to whom Daulat Rao made over the command of the regulars and the civil charge of the territory assigned for their support, on the departure of General de Boigne.

This, it may be remembered, was that Pierre Cuiller (the ex-mariner) who has been so often mentioned in these pages under his assumed style of "General Perron." Extending, as his career does, over the whole period of the existence of the regular corps in Sindhia's service, it is no less interesting from the picture that it shows of an attempt at civil administration in pre-British Hindustan. His case exhibits an epitome, so to speak, of the extremes of fortune to which an adventurer of those days might be liable, and of the peculiar trials awaiting a man of uncultivated character when at last the luck turned and successes came which he had done little to earn and for the enjoyment of which he had made no preparation. An average man he was, of mediocre abilities, without either exceptional merit or conspicuous failings. When Boigne was leaving India, on that indefinite furlough from which he was never to return, he probably acquiesced in the appointment of his successor, estimating him as "a man of plain sense; no talent, but a brave soldier."

But the General's last advice to Sindhia betrayed anxiety as to Perron's political wisdom and judgment;

for he enjoined upon him "never to offend the British, and to discharge his troops sooner than risk a war with that nation."

Like Thomas, the new Commander-in-Chief of the regulars—as has been stated above—was originally a seaman. Coming out with Suffren, he deserted his ship and entered the service as a client of Mr. Sangster, the Scots gun-founder, who procured him a post as sergeant of infantry; and his further promotion was due to his industry, which—according to Smith—was such that "his pleasures arose from the labours of his profession." A resolute plodder like this will always prosper until he comes to be confronted by extraordinary circumstances demanding originality and resource. By great activity and constant attention to duty Perron won his way to the good graces of his superiors; and when old Mahadaji went to Poona in 1792, his time for distinction was at hand.

Sindhia had always been on good terms with Ahalia Bai, the wise and good Lady of Indore, who was faithfully served by Tukaji Holkar as long as she was able to control that rough soldier's zeal. But in 1792 the Bai was breaking, the inroads of devotional austerities anticipating the ravages of years and natural decay. Tukaji now began to assume a freer hand: the absence of Sindhia seemed to give an opportunity; he summoned Ismail Beg to his standard and marched towards Ujain. The readiness of the Beg to fight with any one and in any cause we have already noticed; and thus, on the present summons, he joined the widow of Najaf Kuli in her sand-locked fortress of Kanaund. This was a stronghold walled with clay, a material almost impervious to round-shot; and the nature of the surrounding soil rendered the approach of heavy guns peculiarly difficult; the water-supply, moreover, was deficient; and the shrubs of the surrounding jungle did not afford timber of sufficient scantling to be of use to the works of a besieging army. When Perron was sent against the place, the widow and her champion reckoned upon holding out long enough to allow of Tukaji coming up to the relief. But they were doomed to swift and bitter disappointment. First the Beg tried a sortie, which was driven back with loss. Then the valiant widow—sister of the infamous Pathan Nawab Ghulām Kādar—was killed by a shell upon the rampart. Finally, the men lost confidence in themselves and in the Moghal Jonah who had brought the tempest on them, and began to talk of throwing him overboard. Ismail, getting wind of these mutterings, resolved to be beforehand with his would-be sacrificers, and opened secret negotiations with Perron, who willingly entertained them. The place was surrendered on promise of life to the Beg and his garrison, and the unlucky *sabreur* was removed to the fort at Agra, where he remained a prisoner until his death, about four years later, living an idle life, on a pension of Rs. 600 per mensem, in the house on the highest and most ventilated part of the place, still known as the house of Dan Sah Jat. He was the greatest cavalry leader of the day, and had never been beaten until he encountered the regulars.

When General de Boigne returned to Aligurh, after defeating the main body of the invaders at Lahkairi, he received orders to send to Sindhia, at Poona, a force of 10,000 of these trained foot-soldiers, which was accordingly despatched under the command of Colonel Perron. And when the General returned to Europe in the beginning of 1796, nothing was more natural than that the man who had held the heights above Kardla against his compatriot, the famous Michel Raymond, should be selected to fill the vacancy. The force at the time comprised only three brigades, and Colonel Trimont, who commanded one, died at this very juncture. The choice lay, therefore, between Perron and the remaining Brigadier. This was Colonel Sutherland, never a favourite.

If any question was made, it should have been left to be decided by the retiring General de Boigne, who, however, does not appear to have moved in behalf of the French sailor. The results, in any case, were momentous, involving the fate of Sindhia's dynasty and of the British Empire in Hindustan.[1]

When Perron assumed the command the force was far from being so large as it ultimately became, though probably of sufficient strength for all reasonable uses, trained and inured to battle as it was. Each of the three brigades was composed of ten battalions, each battalion consisting of 400 rank and file, 94 non-commissioned officers, and with a major, captain, and one or two subalterns of European origin. With each were fifty guns, of various calibres for field-service and siege, the bombardiers being Christians and the gunners Hindu or Muslim natives of India. The artillery was guarded by 200 disciplined horsemen. Later, Perron added a fourth brigade, similarly constituted; in 1803, when war was imminent, a fifth was raised; at the time of Lake's advance from Cawnpore, the brigades of Begum Sombre and Filose brought the whole strength of the force to a total of close on 60,000. There was a corps of 500 light horse attached to each brigade, with a contingent of irregular infantry carrying matchlocks fitted with bayonets, a compromise between musketeers and pikemen which was very unlikely to be useful against disciplined troops. The pay of the Christian officers was high: the salary of a lieutenant-colonel, serving north of the Narbada river, was Rs. 2,000 per mensem, besides table-allowance; when sent into the Deccan, an increase of 50 per cent. was made to all. Perron had, in addition to the pay of his rank as General-in-Chief, sufficient profit out of the assigned lands to bring his income up to Rs. 60,000 monthly!

[1] But see extracts in the Appendix, from which we may perhaps conclude that the General would have preferred to be succeeded by Colonel Sutherland.

Nothing is recorded as to military affairs for the next twelve months. Perron lived at the Sahib-Bagh, the house formerly occupied by his predecessor, midway between the city of Koil and the fort of Aligurh; while Colonel du Drenec, who had come over from Holkar's service to that of Sindhia, and now commanded one of the brigades, was provided with quarters in a house in cantonments mentioned above as having been afterwards used as the Court-house of the British District Judge. As to civil administration, the General did as much or as little as he thought good. At Dehli, and within the narrow circle of the sphere now left to the Emperor, his authority was paramount; but his attention was mainly directed to the collection of the revenue, which was done by the help of large bodies of troops kept at hand for the purpose. In the event of recalcitrance on the part of landholders a severe and early example was made, the village of the defaulters being plundered and burned, with bloodshed on occasion. In the department of justice matters were no less summary; there were no rules of procedure and neither Hindu nor Muslim law was properly administered. The suppression of crime was treated as a negligible quantity; the *Amil*, or District Officer, sent in his report on any special case and acted according to such orders as Perron chose to send back. As to rating of land, there was nothing of what has since been known as "Settlement"; the *Amil* took what he could get from the landholder, and the landholder got what he could from the cultivators. No one dared to build a handsome masonry house, or to celebrate a showy wedding, or give silver bracelets or bangles to the females of his family; such things would have only served as signals to the chartered spoiler. The well-to-do accumulated what they dared not enjoy, to bury it underground and often die without having revealed the place of its concealment. Every considerable landholder had a sort of unauthorised custom-house—*Sayar-Chabootra*, as it was called—where goods *in transitu* paid such dues as the rural magnate deemed available. Besides this, he derived an income from shares in the booty taken from travellers by professional gangs of gipsies and predatory tribes. The obstacles to commerce were completed by disbanded soldiers who roamed the country. What wonder if—as in the days of the ancient Deborah—"the highways were unoccupied, the travellers walked through byways." [1]

Perron, as one of our authorities has suggested, thought chiefly of making hay while the sun shone; nevertheless it must be confessed that he was prepared to uphold his position. In 1798, finding a Maratha rival in possession of the palace at Dehli and the person of the Emperor, he sent a force under his compatriot, Colonel Pédron, who sat down before the gates and attempted to effect the reduction by a mixture of bribery and blockade. For the time being he was unsuccessful. When at last the garrison yielded, the charge of the palace and its august inmate was confided to Colonel Drugeon, the gallant conqueror of the old ladies at Kirki; but hardly was this accomplished when a Maratha competitor reappeared at Agra. Perron marched against him in person and took the town; but the castle held out for two months, and its capture cost him 400 men; the trouble did not end until April, 1799. Then followed the campaign against Lakwa Dada and the Dattia Raja of which a brief mention was made in the notice of the ill-starred Bellasis. In all these affairs Perron acquitted himself as an energetic commander; and by the end of the year—like the late Marshal O'Donnell—had not an enemy left, unless he

[1] These facts have been gleaned from various sources, such as the letters of an "Old Resident of Aligurh" in ancient files of the *Dehli Gazette*, and the Statistical Report of Messrs. J. R. Hutchinson and J. W. Sherer, Roorkee, 1856.

failed to conciliate his brother blue-jacket in Hariana. George Thomas, in an independent position, appeared a harbinger of British power; and British power the Frenchman was determined to oppose. This feeling probably accounts for the obstinacy with which Thomas was pursued, as we have already seen, and finally abolished.

By the beginning of 1802 Perron had attained his zenith, having brought all Hindustan into subjection, and being regarded as suzerain by every chief—Hindu or Muslim—from the Sutlej to the Narbada. His demeanour now underwent a total change. Surrounded by flatterers, he gave all his confidence to Frenchmen, like Louis Bourquin, and actually sent one Descartes as Envoy to France to seek the alliance of First-Consul Bonaparte, then on the eve of breaking the short-lived Peace of Amiens.

Some conception of the enormous resources at this time acquired by the whilom man-of-war's man may be formed by reference to a schedule of his possessions annexed to the treaty made with Sindhia at the termination of the war, from which we find that he held personally, in addition to the twenty-seven districts formerly assigned to General de Boigne, seven fiefs (*Jaigirs*) which he had "resumed" from their former owners; four large estates (*Talukas*) in the Dehli territory; twelve districts west of the river Jumna; the *Soobah* of Sahāranpur; yielding—under the crude management then subsisting—an aggregate of over four millions of rupees, say £400,000, per annum. This vast domain was his own absolute property, over and above his official pay and allowances and the whole patronage of four brigades.

Of the manner in which Perron conducted this important part of his administration we obtain a glimpse in the *Memoirs* of James Skinner, to which frequent reference has been made in these pages. Of all his

Brigadiers only one—Colonel Sutherland—appears to have been of British blood, from first to last; and this although a very considerable portion of the battalion-officers, captains, and subalterns were of that class. His selections, dictated partly by natural feelings, were not the less unhappy in the end. "Every low Frenchman," writes the indignant Smith, "every low Frenchman that he advanced, with outrage to others, repaid his unjust preference with ingratitude." That the partiality was not due to superior prowess on the part of the General's compatriots is shown by the "singular fact that, though there were as many French and foreign officers in Sindhia's service as (there were) British subjects, only four French officers were killed during twenty years' service, while fifteen British officers fell in the same space of time." It must be borne in mind that this testimony, though not wilfully dishonest, is from a prejudiced source. Perron may have been injudicious in the disposal of his patronage, but he was a brave and loyal Frenchman, as will be seen hereafter. Bourquin—the champion against Thomas—is a signal instance of a bad choice. Bourquin's inefficiency in that campaign has already been observed, and it led to his temporary supersession as a brigade-commander; but his reinstatement was not long retarded, for in the same year he had charge of the 3rd Brigade, and at the beginning of 1803 he was at Dehli with a second brigade, and on that occasion displayed another side of his versatile baseness. For, fancying that Perron's influence with Sindhia was on the wane, Bourquin availed himself of the opportunity to enter into a conspiracy for ousting the General and obtaining his place. With this object he plundered Perron's banker of nine lakhs of rupees, seduced the men from their allegiance, besieged Colonel Drugeon in the palace, and wrote to the native officers of the cavalry at Aligurh offering them large rewards for the arrest or assassination of General Perron.

But we need not anticipate. For the moment we will leave the General in the command of the army and of the country, with the enjoyment of his vast property and of an apparently impregnable position. His vain struggles and rapid collapse will form the subject of a new chapter.

CHAPTER XII

Perron declines in power—The Treaty of Bassain—Plan of campaign against British—Lake's advance and Perron's surrender—Fight at Dehli and subsequent fortunes of the foreign officers—Campaign closed by battle of Laswāri.

THE dissatisfaction of Bourquin had less excuse than that of Major Smith and his British-born brothers. Yet, if Perron had been in a position to carry out a project for keeping the heart of the Moghal Empire as a preserve for his own countrymen, it would be scarcely a matter for surprise that he should not have neglected the very simple expedient of entrusting at least the higher commands to officers of French nationality. It must have been known to him that the Peace of Amiens was not very likely to last. Lord Wellesley's conduct in 1802 had not been such as to convey to any intelligent observer in India any strong belief in the duration of the arrangement. The First Consul vainly attempted to avail himself of the truce—which he, too, knew to be no more than transitory—by reoccupying and strengthening the French settlements in India; and Admiral Linois appeared off the coast with a squadron of ships carrying important reinforcements. But the vigilant Wellesley, anticipating the coming rupture, refused to allow the Admiral to land at Pondichéri—a high-handed proceeding, perhaps, yet not altogether without justification. For among the archives of that place had turned up a copy of a paper lately prepared for the information of the First Consul by a Lieutenant Le Fèvre, in which the most unblushing calumnies were heaped upon the alleged treatment of the

Emperor by the British, coupled with plans for the extirpation of "that unprincipled race." Considering that the Emperor had been for some time in durance, with a French force in Dehli and a French officer in the palace, the statements in this document were not wanting in ingenious audacity; and it is conceivable that they may have been supplied by Perron.

In the meantime that officer was doing a great deal to undermine his own position. Having disgusted one section of his European followers without making any very valuable body of support among the other, he was also alienating the Maratha chiefs; of whom more than one had been superseded by Perron in promotion, and naturally had long been regarding the prosperity of the foreigner with jealous eyes. He had, moreover, attracted the odium of Sindhia's father-in-law and chief favourite, the notorious Shirji Rao, Ghatkai; and Sindhia himself was learning to give ear to hostile representations. Then followed an event which did not tend to allay the chief's ill-humour and general perplexity: the Peshwa having concluded a treaty—called "of Bassain"—by which Lord Wellesley secured for his Government what he termed "an absolute ascendancy in the councils of Poona"—and, in Sindhia's expressed opinion, "taken the turban off his head." As yet Sindhia had not dared to throw himself heartily into those anti-British efforts to which Perron had been long urging him; and now Perron had fallen into such disgrace that, on the 25th March, 1803, he was insulted by Sindhia in open Durbar at Ujain. About this time the effect of all this upon the General's mind had been to lead him into correspondence with Lake, the British officer preparing at Cawnpore for an advance upon Aligurh; and on the 27th of the same month Lord Wellesley wrote that "Mr. Perron's departure would be an event promising much advantage to our power in India."

But if Perron, smarting under anxiety and disgrace, for

a moment entertained thoughts of abandoning his agitated master, the mood only lasted as long as the master's own indecision. About the 1st July it became evident to him that Sindhia was not likely to continue on friendly terms with the Calcutta Government. Only one month before Perron, returned from Ujain, was living as a private person at Aligurh, preparing to make over the command of the army with the civil administration into the charge of Ambaji Ainglia, who had been ordered up from Central India to take his place; before July was over he had been restored to power, and was discovered to be sending round a circular to native chiefs and Princes, in Sindhia's name, inviting them to form a general league and active combination against the British. At the same time Lake, at Cawnpore, was warned to be ready. "The reduction of Sindhia's power on the north-west frontier of Hindustan"—Cawnpore was then the frontier station —"is an important object in proportion to the probability of a war with France."

If it should now be thought far-fetched to look for French leanings among the native Princes, the thought is easily corrected by remembering the case of Tippu at Seringapatam in the earlier days of the still existing administration. After the capture of that city in 1799, an examination of the late Sultan's State papers revealed a complete series of documents to show that Tippu had been inviting help from General Malartic, Governor of Mauritius; that volunteers had been invited, and that officers and men commissioned, or at least sanctioned, by the Directory had, in considerable number, landed at Mangalore and gone on to Seringapatam. There, like Perron in the North, they had not been received without jealousy by the native officials. "Your Highness is not ignorant," so it was written in a memorial by Mir Yusuf, of the Revenue Board of Mysore, "that it is the custom of the French to promise much, but to perform little." But Tippu comments :—

"If the theatre of war were in France, would not the God-given State" (*L'Etat, c'est moi*) "do all in his power to assist? And surely the Frenchmen cannot do less." The Frenchmen in Mysore did much less: yet here was another Indian chief trusting them again; and the French nation at home was now far more powerful and under far more audacious and formidable guidance than in the days of the moribund Directory. In point of fact, the danger was real and imminent, though much mitigated by two unforeseen occurrences: the first was the death of Paul, the Russian Czar, on whom the First Consul had depended as ally and cat's-paw; the second being the necessity under which Bonaparte appeared to find himself for taking active steps against the negroes in San Domingo. This expedition for the moment appeared likely to absorb the whole spare resources of the First Consul; but Wellesley did not know of it, and may well have believed that an enemy like Bonaparte would not neglect any opportunity of injuring Britain that might be afforded by the alliance of a French party in India.

It was, undoubtedly, under such persuasions that Wellesley would have been glad to procure "the retirement of Mr. Perron." And the overtures made for that purpose must have inflated the vanity to which the General had shown himself subject and created exaggerated notions of his own importance. Sindhia, too, now that he had at last resolved upon resistance, must have felt that he could not afford to quarrel with his most successful military subordinate, the conqueror of Ismail and Holkar, of the Nizam and the famous General Raymond. So the General resumed his command, though not without danger from the competitive rivalry of Ambaji.

Nor were the possible consequences without a certain element of hopefulness. The British forces advancing into Hindustan and the Deccan were but small numerically; and the majority of their men were no better in blood and quality than the good regular troops trained by Sindhia's officers and victors in so many hard fights. The combination submitted to Sindhia was—on paper—extremely imposing. The plan formed was this:—

The Rohilas, once conquered by the British for the Nawab of Oudh, were now to enter the domains of that potentate, while Ambaji co-operated in the Lower Duāb. Daulat Rao in person was to fall on the Nizam, that ancient enemy of all Marathas. Holkar undertook to ravage Benares and Bihār, while the fertile delta of Bengal was to be the prey of the Nāgpur Bhonsala, then known as the "Raja of Berar."

The forces on which the confederates were to depend comprised twelve brigades of regulars with guns in proportion; a large staff of European and Eurasian officers; a force of heavy cavalry, with predatory horse—of the Pindari type—reckoned at 125,000 lances. On the other side was the resolute Wellesley, telling his Generals that "an effort against Sindhia and Berar was the best possible preparation for the renewal of the war with France."

The moment of crisis approached. The Treaty of Amiens had pleased no one in England; the Tories were never reconciled to the Revolution, the Whigs objected to the First Consul for the opposite reason that he had destroyed the Republic. Bonaparte himself hardly disguised his feeling that it was only a temporary armistice. When, therefore, the British Cabinet—suspecting hostile designs in Egypt—refused to restore the Island of Malta to the Knighthood to whom it properly belonged, Bonaparte was prepared with his well-known scene with the Ambassador Whitworth, on which the latter applied for his passports and returned to England. Letters of marque were issued by the British Cabinet on 16th May; on the 3rd of the following month French troops entered the Kingdom of Hanover; the news of the rupture of the peace reached India overland. But, even before he learned that the war had been actually renewed,

Wellesley had already addressed an ultimatum to Daulat Rao Sindhia, of whose increasing hostility he was informed by Colonel Collins, his envoy with that chief.

It was about this time that Perron was reinstated, and that he issued the circular to which reference has already been made. Sindhia at the same date maintained close relations with the Raja of Berar, contrary to an express clause in the ultimatum of Collins; and that officer—under conditional instructions—quitted Sindhia's camp on August 3rd.

The military power which the Calcutta Government had to oppose to the formidable confederacy by which it appeared to be menaced was of moderate strength, to say the most of it. Its power lay in the quality of its men and of their leaders. Lake advanced from Cawnpore at the head of 10,000 men, of all arms, only three cavalry corps and one battalion of foot being British soldiers; the remainder were, however, good native troops, officered by Europeans. About 3,500 men were assembled at Allahabad for operations in Bundelkhand; 5,200 were got ready to encounter the Berar army in Orissa; while Sir A. Wellesley and Stevenson were directed to enter the Deccan with 17,000 men, supported by a strong reserve in the Province of Madras, or "the Carnatic."

Lake received his last orders on August 17th, after he had already left Cawnpore, and the talents and resources of General Perron were now to be put to the proof. If he had the army in hand and were true to himself, he had the means of a glorious resistance; that he desired to do his duty is the opinion alike of Skinner and of Smith, though the latter—writing, however, after the event—has pointed out the weaknesses which affected his efforts. What followed is matter of familiar knowledge to the student of history; let us look at it, as best we may, in its more intimate relations and as it appeared to persons on the spot.

Perron's first and most honourable act was to send to his Dehli banker an unlimited credit in favour of the royal family, with instructions to the effect that a letter should be sent to Lake in the Emperor's name forbidding the advance of the British army; Du Drenec was ordered up from Malwa with his brigade; and Perron announced to all and sundry his intention to stand by the cause of Sindhia unless he should be regularly relieved of his charge. He also took care to send a large force of cavalry, under Captain Fleury (one of his best French officers), to lay waste the country to the south-east and hamper Lake's advance. Having taken these measures, he could do no more than await the event.

The stars in their courses fought against him; the measures all failed. The Emperor, indeed, signed the required address to Lake; but he sent an agent to camp, at the same time, to explain that he had only written at the dictation of the French officers and did not mean a word of it. Hundreds of sepoys, knowing that their wives and families were in the power of the British in their homes in Bihār and Allahabad, deserted daily; and the British-born officers, who had been particularly warned, by a Proclamation of the Governor-General, not to bear arms against their own King, were in many instances ready to lay down their commissions. Fleury gained the day in a skirmish with Lake's picquets, but was soon taken prisoner; Du Drenec never got further than Mathra, where his surrender to Vandeleur has been already noticed. On the 27th, a couple of British officers in Perron's service applied to him for their discharge, on which the General ordered all the rest to leave the camp. On the following day Lake came up and found the troubled Frenchman drawn up with the remainder of his men before the fort of Aligurh.

The scene that ensued savours of comic opera. Lake sent out a reconnoitring party of cavalry, with what were called "galloper-guns"—a kind of precursor of the horse-artillery of later days; and Perron's Maratha horsemen dispersed before the shots fired at them. Skinner, who had at that time no particular reason to love his father's nation, and whose character it was to be faithful to his salt, thought that he saw in his General's distress an opportunity of getting the dismissal order of the previous day reversed. Perceiving Perron bare-headed and riding about endeavouring to rally his horse-men, Skinner ran to him, seized the bridle of the charger, and made an offer of service to his distracted General.

"Ah! no," said the General. "All is over. These fellows have behaved badly; do not ruin yourself. Go over to the English; it is all up with us."

Skinner, renewing his assurances of devotion, was now told plainly that confidence was at an end. On his becoming urgent, Perron shook him off, riding away with the repeated cry:—

"Goodbye, Monsieur Skinner! No trust, no trust."

That night the General departed to Hatras, leaving the fort of Aligurh in the hands of his son-in-law, Colonel Pédron, whom he enjoined to remember that he represented the honour of France and must hold out to the last extremity (which, be it added, he did). On arrival at Hatras, Perron learned that Ambaji was coming up to take the command out of his hands. With this information, and the knowledge that Bourquin was betraying him at Dehli, Perron lost all heart and gave himself up to General Lake at Sasni. He was kindly treated there, and passed into a peaceful life in British India, where he spent some time settling his affairs; and the fact, revealed by papers in the possession of the family, that he received several friendly letters from Daulat Rao Sindhia after his retirement, seems enough to disprove the insinuations against his fidelity in which some writers have sought to bury his name.

General Perron ultimately returned to France in 1806 with a considerable fortune, being then in his 54th year.

He bought the Château of Frasnes in the Vendôme country, not very far from the place which he had left, thirty-five years before, as a humble workman ; here he passed many years of quiet beneficence, like his old commander, Boigne, with whom he maintained a constant correspondence ; and here he died in his 80th year, and was buried in the neighbouring cemetery. He left two sons, both of whom died without issue ; his daughters made excellent marriages, one—Countess de la Rochefoucauld—surviving till 1892.

Of Perron's loyalty of character there ought to be no question. Even Smith, who considered that the French Commander had dealt unjustly with himself and the other British-born officers of the service, does not hesitate to justify the General's conduct in 1803. "I do not think," he writes the very next year, "that [Perron] wanted either sense, prudence, or principle, in quitting Sindhia's service when he did." James Mill (vol. vi., p. 502) is even more favourable. It was the gift of fortune that he was able to leave with life and property ; and in so doing he did but his duty to himself and his family without any harm to a not too faithful employer. In a paper never published, for the use of which I am indebted to the General's great-grandson,[1] he writes in convincing language to all who know the facts : "The successive treacheries of Bourquin and Pédron, and the suspicious conduct of almost all the other officers, had inspired the natives with such distrust of Europeans that our lives were in hourly danger. . . . For myself, I only saved mine by great sacrifices of money." He had, moreover, been superseded by Sindhia's orders, if not actually cashiered, at the time when Lake advanced from Cawnpore. This much justice is due to a man who, with no such

[1] For information about General Perron I am indebted to the Marquis de Brantes, Captain in the 1st Regiment of Chasseurs in the French Army, whose grandmother, Countess of Montesquiou Fézensac, was the General's eldest daughter.

advantages of birth and breeding as those possessed by his predecessor, yet attained to equal distinction and only failed by reason of events for which he was scarcely answerable. We have seen something of what he did when in power; of his character and conduct in retreat those who knew him speak in the highest terms, attesting alike his rectitude, his simplicity, and his wide charity.

The fate of the other non-British officers may be told in a few lines. The faithless Bourquin—who commanded at Dehli—led his two brigades against Lake after the fall of Aligurh, which he might have seriously hindered had he chosen to go to Pédron's relief and taken the small British force between two fires. Even without aid, Pédron made a good fight; and the assault was not accomplished without a loss of 260 to the British, the 76th Foot alone having 73 killed or wounded.

On the 11th September Bourquin crossed the river Jumna and took up a position on the plain between Dehli and the Hindun, having with him a force of twelve battalions, nearly seventy guns, and 5,000 horses. The advance guard of the British had just come up, fatigued by a long march, and were preparing to pitch their camp; but Lake took them on as soon as he ascertained the near approach of the enemy, whose position he at once attacked in the fearless old fashion. His whole available strength consisted of the decimated 76th, a few corps of sepoys, a regiment of British Dragoons, and another of native cavalry. The latter went on ahead and were exposed to a terrible fire from Bourquin's batteries, while they sat on their horses awaiting the arrival of the infantry; Lake's horse was shot under him. When the infantry came up, they were formed in line and taken against the enemy's batteries with shouldered muskets, led by the Commander-in-Chief himself. Drawn up behind their guns, the regulars offered a sullen defence, unsupported by the cavalry; the British attacked the batteries with fixed bayonets, and Bourquin with his staff galloped from the field; the British line broke into columns, the cavalry charged through the intervals, and the enemy's resistance soon ceased. The French officers surrendered a few days later.

In the following month came the turn of Agra, held by Sutherland's brigade and further defended by seven battalions who were encamped outside with twenty-six guns. The walled town was taken, after a bloody struggle, on the 10th October; a week later the garrison asked for terms and were allowed to capitulate. Du Drenec arrived from Agra, with our old friend Smith, in charge of Colonel Vandeleur of the 8th Dragoons—afterwards killed at Laswāri.

The European officers had now been all taken, or had surrendered of their own free will under the Proclamation. But there was a large part of their followers remaining to be dealt with yet. Raja Ambaji had been appointed to relieve Perron, as already said, but he too had been in treaty with Lake on his own behalf; so much so, indeed, that in the month of October he had been expected to embrace the British protection on certain conditions. But the conditions were not carried out by him; and Ambaji continued his slow progress northward. By the end of October he had reached a village between Alwar and Agra, known in history as Laswāri—Naswāri the correct word. Having been here joined by Du Drenec's command and by the *débris* of the Dehli garrison, Ambaji now had a fine force of seventeen regular battalions with seventy-one guns and 5,000 horse. Lake, pushing on—as was his custom—at the head of his cavalry, found his army well posted in a semicircle of which the Mewāt hills were the arc and a deep stream the chord. It was about sunrise on the morning of November 1st when Lake forded the water and charged the enemy's lines without waiting for the infantry to come up. He had about 3,000 men with him, of whom little over a quarter were European Dragoons. Three times did these fearless cavaliers ride through the high grass jungle, charge the guns, and break the line of the regulars, while the Maratha horsemen looked on according to their use and wont. Vandeleur was killed; horses and men became weary; the guns could not be brought away; Lake had to retire to the other side of the water and give his men rest and food. In the meantime the British infantry arrived; and, after an attempt at negotiation on the part of Ambaji had failed, the action was renewed. Never did British troops behave with a steadier valour, seldom did British troops encounter a more worthy foe. The General had another horse killed, and his son got a severe wound while assisting his father to mount a fresh charger; General Ware's head was taken off by a round shot. At length the guns were taken; Ambaji, dismounting from his elephant, galloped away on horseback; the resistance declined after his disappearance, and finally ceased, with a loss of 7,000 men and all the guns. The British loss in that stubborn contest amounted to 13 officers and over 800 men.

With the battles of Asai and Argaon in the South, the war ceased, and Sindhia concluded the *Annus Mirabilis* by a treaty in which he engaged to employ no Europeans or Americans without the knowledge and consent of the British Government.

Thus ended, three years after the beginning of a new century, the career and calling which had given such a romantic hue to the generally prosaic age just expired. Two of the officers, however, lived to distinguish themselves in the British service, of whom one came from the army of Sindhia and one from that of Holkar.

CHAPTER XIII

James Skinner, Colonel and C.B.—His rise, transfer to British service, subsequent good work and death.

WE have seen how James Skinner attempted to stand by Sindhia's French General in his last attitude of defence, and it may be asked why he, a man whose name sounds so English, and who died a Colonel and Companion of the Bath in the British service, should have been willing to run all hazards against the soldiers of his mother-country. The explanation must be sought in the peculiar conditions of his origin and early life.

Skinner was born about 1778, his father being a subaltern in the British Army in Bengal, and his mother a Rājput lady with whom the subaltern had a transient intimacy. After an attempt to apprentice the boy to a Calcutta printer, which entirely failed owing to his restless and venturesome nature, the father was fain to let him take his own wilful way, which led him to the wild life of a private spearman, ending by a subaltern's commission in one of Sindhia's regular regiments of infantry. He served in the little war against George Thomas, and we are indebted to him for anecdotes such as have been already related. Up to the date of Lake's advance Skinner had lived amongst his men, and had an ignorance of the British as profound as theirs. He had also, as it seems, a special grudge against the race to which his father belonged, which was shared by others in a like position to his own. Brought up by native mothers whom the temporary partners had often

COLONEL JAMES SKINNER, C.B.

(1778–1841.)

From the Memoir by Baillie Fraser.

deserted, their sympathies were with the people of the country. Skinner, for one, desired nothing better, at this time, than to strike a blow for Sindhia, whose salt he had eaten for seven years, ever since he came to man's estate. This Perron's irritation and suspicious condition would not allow; and we have seen that officer riding distractedly without a hat, and bidding Skinner to "go over to the English."

At the end of August accordingly he came into the British camp, with some companions in a like plight. They approached the General's tent with fear and trembling, not knowing how they would be received; but Lake was good to the lads and promised them employment. Skinner had even then too high a sense of honour to accept any duty which might involve him in warfare against his old master, Daulat Rao Sindhia; but Lake was taken with him and gave him police-work on the road towards Cawnpore. Skinner soon raised a body of patrol horse, with whom he took post at Sikandrabad, ten miles east of Bulandshahr, in a former cantonment of Perron's army; and from that centre he made expeditions in support of order, which occasionally assumed serious proportions. Of these enterprises of pith and moment History records one against the fort of Malagurh, four miles north of Bulandshahr, held by a Maratha brigand named Madhu Rao, who sent Skinner a peremptory message inviting him to vacate his post and leave the District. Skinner immediately marched against Malagurh, laid siege to the fort, and soon compelled the Maratha to surrender. His most distant expedition was across the Ganges into what is now the Bijnore District, where—at a place called Afzalgurh—fifteen miles from Nagina—Skinner met and defeated the Pathan adventurer, Amir Khan, afterwards to become such a thorn in the side of Lake. At length open war broke out between the British and Jaswant Rao Holkar. That chieftain had been an old enemy of Sindhia, so Skinner had no scruples in acting against him. Recruiting was easy among Perron's former Moghal horse, and Skinner was soon at the head of a body of cavalry with which he accompanied Lake's heroic marches; in these, British Dragoons—after some months of training—succeeded in driving Amir Khan into Central India and running Holkar to earth in the Punjab. Skinner having adopted a curious kind of canary-coloured uniform, it is to this day perpetuated in the corps by which his "yellow-boys" are represented. It is a wonderful item in the always marvellous record of Anglo-Indian warfare, that British cavalry, with such associates, learned a speed and endurance which ultimately made them too nimble for their subtle prey. With a saddle-bag containing a handful of meal for food, a blanket, and a brass pot for all baggage, each grooming his own horse after a long march, "Mounted Tommy," with his galloper guns, kept up an emulous companionship with the canary-coloured sowars. They chased Holkar and his Pathan associate across the Duāb, crossed the Ganges at Anupshahr, relieved the beleaguered residents of Moradabad and Bareilly, surprised the Maratha camp at Fatehgurh, expelled the Pathan with the loss of 20,000 of his Pindaris, and drove Holkar to a momentary asylum at Jodhpur.[1] Thus passed the year 1804; in the following year the Maratha chief tempted fortune once more, leaving Jodhpur and heading for the Punjab, where he hoped to find an ally in the young Ranjit Singh, then engaged in founding a principality at Lahore. Lake and Skinner at once resumed the initiative, and followed him up so briskly that by the 19th December Holkar, being run into before he could reach Lahore, was obliged to submit to Lake's terms and end the war.

In the peaceful days of "non-intervention" under Sir George Barlow, Skinner beat his sabre into a pruning-hook and settled down as an agriculturist on a large scale

[1] The British regiments were the 8th, 27th, and 29th Dragoons.

in Hariana, where he had once, in a more humble capacity, made war upon the gallant Sailor-Prince, George Thomas. He was employed in settling the Districts for several years, and rewarded with the grant of no less than sixty-seven fine farms in and around the lands of Hánsi; but he also held an estate in the District of Bulandshahr, at a place called Bilaspur, where a good house and garden are to this day possessed by his descendants. In 1815 Skinner and his Yellow-boys bore an honourable part in the operations of Lord Moira—afterwards Marquess of Hastings—against the Pindari marauders; and for this he was rewarded by the publicly expressed thanks of the Governor-General and Commander-in-Chief, and of several General officers. Similar honours were conferred on him after operations against Arab mercenaries who broke out at Poona in 1819; and that—with but one exception—was the last of Skinner's active service. His corps now amounted to no less than 3,000 sabres, of which one-third was about this time paid off and disbanded, while another part was posted at Nimuch, in Rajputāna, under his brother Robert, the remaining 1,000 men going into cantonments at Hánsi with their old commandant. He had long enjoyed the distinguished friendship of the able and genial Sir John Malcolm—mentioned as employed in the delicate duty of disbanding the legion of Michel Raymond in 1798; and by Malcolm's powerful aid he about this date obtained a perpetual and heritable assignment of the estates in Hariana: these had originally been given to him for the maintenance of his men, under the old quasi-feudal system mentioned in our notices of Sombre and Boigne. Bilaspur appears to have been his own property from the first.

In 1822 Skinner once more visited Calcutta, where he had, as a boy, thrown down his composing-stick to trail a pike in Upper India; here he was made much of and bid to return to Hánsi and re-engage his men, who had been disbanded three years before. The times were again becoming troubled; Lord Amherst was preparing for war with Burma; good officers and faithful native soldiers were at a premium. In no long time employment came to Skinner and his Yellow-boys once more.

The period of the first Burmese War was marked by one of those strange political epidemics to which India seems always liable. A sort of magnetic storm brooded over the land, causing unrest and reaction. The upper provinces were full of soldiers whose occupation was gone, and whose habits forbade their finding new work in peaceful fields. The police force was unable to keep such people in order, being itself in a state of imperfect organisation; the administration of justice was imperfect and universally unpopular; worst of all, the settlement of the land—always the corner-stone of the Indian social system—was crude, corrupt and unworkable. Local disturbances ensued; from the Cis-Sutlej country, on the north-west, to the Duāb of the Gangetic valley the troops were constantly on the move to preserve order. In Alwar and in Jaipur the Rājput clansmen were at deadly feud among themselves; and matters were now to be complicated by events that were arising in the famous Jat State, whose capital was at Bhurtpur, imperfectly subdued by Lake in 1804.

The details belong to general history. Here we have only to notice a broad outline. A disputed succession had occurred in the Jat State, the Raja on his death-bed having procured the recognition of his infant son by the paramount power, while his brother attempted to supplant the youthful heir. The Governor-General's Agent, the wise and gallant Sir David Ochterlony, considering that the child's life was in danger from the ambition of the uncle, reported accordingly to Calcutta and mobilised the troops at his disposal. This appeared to be succeeding; the usurping uncle offered to come to

Ochterlony at Dehli and to put the young Raja in his keeping.

Unfortunately, there was the Calcutta Council still to deal with, and that august body, thinking itself better informed than the experienced soldier-statesman on the spot, resolved on "making some arrangement by which Sir D. Ochterlony should retire from active employment."[1] A harsh letter was accordingly despatched to the Agent, rebuking him for what he had done and ordering him to "remand to their cantonments" all the troops that had been called into the field. The indignant veteran laid down his appointment and died; Metcalfe was sent to succeed him; and on arriving wrote to the Council to say that vigorous action ought to be immediately taken. Upon this Lord Amherst declared that his views were "materially altered"; and with the assent of the Council sent Metcalfe powers to act according to his judgment. The policy of Sir David was renewed; but in the meantime the usurper had strengthened his defences and largely augmented the strength of his garrison. Two strong divisions of the Indian army were now launched at the almost impregnable place, which consisted of a walled town and interior citadel, before which Lake's efforts had entirely failed twenty years before. An example was felt by Metcalfe to be loudly demanded: Jaipur and Alwar were ready to rise; Sindhia was in evil mood; the unrest of the Southern Marathas displayed ominous signs; "we might," so an eye-witness wrote at the time, "look in vain for one friendly independent neighbour, disposed to succour or even to forbear."

Upon this momentous scene our old adventurer now entered, to fight once more, and for the last time, in behalf of his benefactors. His second-in-command was Major William Fraser, of the Civil Service, who held an administrative post in Hariana, but had elected to take

[1] Mr. Secretary Swinton to Sir C. Metcalfe, 10th April, 1852.

the field as a military man on this occasion.[1] The place was taken, after a five weeks' siege, in which cavalry were usefully employed to make a cordon round the town; Skinner's horse, particularly, co-operated by taking possession of the dam, by cutting which the waters of a neighbouring lake could have been discharged into the ditch by whose deep bed the town was surrounded. Fraser drove off the enemy's cavalry and saved the dam, the enemy thus being left without a moat; and the mine by which the great bastion was destroyed was rendered easily possible. The sowars were also constantly useful in collecting forage and escorting convoys; and some of them were even named in orders to take part in the storming-party, though the assault was ultimately delivered without them.

In 1826 the Colonel and his men returned to Hánsi; and Skinner was soon afterwards gratified by the bestowal of a Lieutenant-Colonel's commission in the royal army and the Third Class Order of the Bath. He had still many years left in which to enjoy his well-earned honours, and he lived an active existence at Hánsi, much esteemed by natives and Europeans, and bringing up a large family, one of whom followed his father's footsteps and became in his turn a commander of cavalry. Amongst other good works, the old soldier built a large and costly church at Dehli. Although in his latter days quite English in his habits, he used the Persian language by preference when he had to write at length. When the unhappy heir of the Sombres was contemplating his visit to Europe in 1836, the Colonel addressed him in a Persian ode strongly dissuasive of the step. He also wrote in that idiom the *Memoirs* afterwards translated by Baillie Fraser. He died in 1841, and was buried in the precincts of his church at Dehli.

A very analogous case was that of W. L. Gardner,

[1] Fraser was afterwards murdered by Nawab Shams-ud-din of Lohāru, who was hanged for the crime.

whose adventurous career has been well summarised, by Mr. Manners Chichester, in the *Dictionary of National Biography* (vol. xx.). Some MS. matter having come into the hands of the present writer from a private source, it has been thought that a few additional particulars might be acceptable; the more so because an illustrious writer has drawn general attention to the case by giving to the world a burlesque picture—*mutato nomine*—calculated to give an erroneous idea of a good and gallant officer who had, indeed, many experiences which might deserve such an epithet as "tremendous," but who, nevertheless, was in character a very different man from the "Major Gahagan" of Thackeray. An Irish Major, indeed, who served under Holkar; but who did useful work in India with calm reticence, waiting patiently for opportunity, and well content to live and die with honour and without honours.

CHAPTER XIV

Colonel W. L. Gardner—Early life and scene with Holkar—Retirement at Khāsganj, and valuable service in the Gurkha War of 1815—Foundation of the Bengal Cavalry.

BORN of a good Irish stock, and nephew of a distinguished naval officer, William Linnæus Gardner entered the royal army at the age of eighteen, and in due course obtained a company in the 30th Foot, now 1st Battalion East Lancashire. In 1795 he took part in the ill-advised and worse-conducted landing of French Royalists in Quiberon Bay, where Gardner not only smelt powder, but became acquainted with a nobleman who subsequently became Governor-General with the title of Marquess of Hastings and under whom he was to serve again in India many years later.

He joined his regiment in that country about a year after this, but found no scope for his martial ardour. It was at this otherwise uneventful time that Sir John Shore—afterwards Lord Teignmouth—had been unlucky enough to offend the officers of the army, as we noticed in dealing with Bellasis. Whether on that account, or for mere restlessness, Gardner also resigned his commission to seek employ in native service. He engaged under Tukaji Holkar, then almost at the end of his career, one in which he had never manifested much hostility against the British, and had, indeed, generally acted as the subordinate of the wise and good widow of the founder of the State, the celebrated Ahalya Bai. Soon after this, however, Tukaji died, having survived his mistress for a short time, during which he had carried on the administration at Indore; and his place fell to an illegitimate son—the brave but ferocious Jaswant Rao, of whom we have already had glimpses. Hence all sorts of trouble arose; so that it was not long before the new officer found work to do.

The first efforts of Jaswant Rao, after getting rid of certain competitors to the succession, was to punish Daulat Rao Sindhia, who had been profiting by the domestic troubles of the clan. It was not, however, till late in 1799 that all was settled, and the regulars—under Colonel Du Drenec—were ready to act under the new chief. The first engagement was that fierce fight with Sindhia's army, commanded by Hessing, of which something has been said above; it was fought at Ujain and ended in the defeat of Hessing, who was the only one of the white officers on Sindhia's side that was not either killed or captured.

But the tables were soon turned. Ere long the unlucky Holkar lost a battle that cost him his camp, his guns, and his capital city of Indore. Du Drenec deserted to the winning side, but several of the British-born officers remained faithful to Holkar, and Gardner was one. Their fidelity soon met with a cruel recompense. On October 25, 1802, they underwent a fresh trial, when Sindhia made a final bid for power in the Deccan, but were at last completely victorious, though a gallant young comrade, named Harding, lost his life. This engagement occurred near Poona, the possession of which city was one of the spoils. The Peshwa fled to British protection, having taken sides with Sindhia's General; and the beginning was made of that train of negotiation that was to end in the Treaty of Bassain and the dawn of the new Empire of India.

Holkar now changed his policy, joining with Sindhia in machinations against the British—mentioned in relating the fall of Perron—which produced a combination of alarming appearance as long as it was confined to talk. As we have seen, these plans were rudely shattered by the British Governor and his Generals before Holkar had committed himself by any act of overt hostility. Whilst he was still wavering, this chief was disposed to try whether he could make terms for himself, and it struck him that Gardner was a man fitted, by character and social standing, to plead his cause with Lake. Gardner, who was now married to a Muslim lady, daughter of the Nawab of Cambay—was ready to undertake the mission to the British camp; and, being furnished with due credentials, he departed, leaving his family under the chief's protection.

The emissary was, doubtless, honest, but the principal was probably insincere—that at least was the feeling in Lake's mind; after some discussion the negotiation came to nought, and Gardner took his leave and rode back to Holkar's camp. Dismounting at the door of the Durbar tent, he entered the presence of the chief, who was sitting on the floor propped on cushions, and, in all probability, more or less intoxicated—his "constant custom of an afternoon." Around him sat his parasites, with the officers by whom he was attended in hours of business, and Gardner was bid to give an account of his proceedings. Holkar was annoyed at his envoy's ill-success, and, although he knew that this was not the fault of the envoy, he began to vent his spleen at the delay, which he said was so caused. From complaints he got to insolent upbraiding, winding-up with an assurance that, had not Gardner returned when he did, the wall of his private tents would have been thrown down by order. This last insult was, like the rest, a mere piece of drunken ill-temper; but the British gentleman took it for a studied provocation. He knew that the chief's mind had been filled with sinister anxieties as to the fidelity of his European officers, many of whom, indeed, he ultimately put to death. Gardner's own life now trembled in the scales of Fate. Indignation at the double affront to his fidelity and to his family overpowered the prudence that is seldom very strong in a European provoked by an Asiatic. "Drawing my sword," he used afterwards to relate, "I attempted to cut Holkar down, but was prevented by those about him. Ere they had recovered from their amazement, I rushed from the tent, sprang upon my horse, and was soon out of reach of my pursuers." The incident was followed by the murder of Vickers and his comrades.

After this hare-brained exploit—which certainly vies with the most doughty deeds of Major Gahagan—our adventurer had some further wild experiences. In his flight he fell into the power of the Peshwa's intriguing brother, Amrit Rao, by whom he was invited to bear arms against the British in the Deccan. Gardner, refusing, was bound to a cot and left for execution; but even this did not exhaust his resources or shake his high resolve. Being ere long unbound and directed to march with a guard, he took occasion, on passing over a cliff, to throw himself into the water below, by a fall of fifty feet. He then swam down the stream until his guard had been eluded, assumed the disguise of a grass-cutter, and finally—after some further wanderings—arrived in the British camp. General Lake accorded him a kind reception, and commissioned him to command the cavalry of the Maharaja of Jaipur, an ally of the British. In that capacity Gardner bore a distinguished part in the calamitous retreat of Colonel Monson in 1804. Five years later Gardner was directed to raise a corps of cavalry, for whose maintenance he was to have the estate of Khāsganj, in the Etah District. He was soon relieved from anxiety on the score of his wife: Holkar either had a qualm of conscience or was unwilling to offend her father, the Nawab; the lady was allowed to depart unscathed, and she presently joined her lord at Khāsganj, which was to be their home for many years to come, and where they finally died within a few weeks one of the other.

But before finally retiring into private life, Gardner had still some useful work to his hand. The papers above referred to bear a special reference to this affair, which happened during Moira's Nepalese War, say between 1814 and 1816, as will be found related in our next chapter. The Governor-General was of that Anglo-Irish race which, from Sir Eyre Coote to the Roberts of to-day, has given so many soldiers and statesmen to the Empire. As Colonel Rawdon, he had held the post of Adjutant-General, and had learnt something of the art of war; at Bunker Hill, in 1775, he had rescued his Captain—George Harris of the 5th Fusiliers—at a moment when the future conqueror of Seringapatam was lying apparently lifeless, with a bullet in his head[1]; in 1793 he had succeeded, on the death of his father, to the newly-created earldom of Moira, and had become a friend of the Prince of Wales. In 1806 he was made Master-General of the Ordnance, and was employed in political dealings by his royal friend, now Regent. In 1812 the excellent Minto had intimated an intention of laying down his office—there was no five-years' rule in those days, nor till long after—and, before the time had come, Moira was sent out to take charge from him. He landed in October, 1813, a shocking example, it must be admitted, of Court patronage.

Nevertheless, as events were to develop themselves, this act of flagrant interference with the East India Company and its Governor-General was to be abundantly justified. The undistinguished Staff-Officer, society-man, and courtier, thus unexpectedly promoted to what was the most exalted and trying position in the British Empire, proved—though an ungrateful posterity hardly recollects the fact—to be chief integrator of the

[1] Lushington, *Life of Lord Harris*, chap. vi.

sway of Britain in the East. Things were already in a similar state of unsettlement to what has been already noticed as existing some ten years later; a state the recurrence of which is one of the main apologies for the appearance of British aggressiveness in the Indian peninsula. The anarchy which had been for a moment got under by Lake and Wellesley was in movement again, like a buried Titan. In Central India the Pindari marauders were abroad; Rajputāna, bleeding to death under the hands of Sindhia and Amir Khan, was feebly calling for deliverance; Oudh was a scene of misgovernment and insecurity; Rohilkhand and the Duāb were disturbed by robber-barons.

As soon as he was fairly instructed in what was on foot, the new Governor announced his intentions: "our object ought to be to make the British Government paramount, in reality if not declaredly" (*Memorandum* of February 6, 1814). With this intention, in his sixtieth year, the veteran set out on a tour in Upper India, hoping against hope that he was not on the edge of "a war more general than any that we have hitherto encountered," and that an invasion by the Nepalese was not to be added to his other tribulations.

It was in this instant of anxiety that Gardner found his opportunity. The beginning of 1814 saw him preparing to enter the Nepalese territory, not as an invader, but in the peaceful capacity of a hunter and fisher, accompanying his cousin, the Hon. Edward Gardner (Assistant Resident at Dehli), on a sporting expedition to the Dehra Dun, then held by the Nepalese. Edward, however, could not go at present, and in April the gallant Major wrote to him from Dehra, where he had got himself into a nest of human hornets. The place was held by an officer of Gurkhas—they are there still, but no longer enemies—who adopted an attitude of anger at Gardner's intrusion; for a moment, he was in some danger. Luckily, the Mahunt of the Sikh Temple—"the Bishop,"

Gardner calls him—was friendly; and by this prelate's influence the sportsman was at last allowed to depart in peace, instead of being shot as a spy.

Open war with Nepal came in November and proved a more serious affair than any one had looked for. Like our mountaineer foes of later days, the Highlanders of the north-east frontier were energetic adversaries upon their native heights. Colonel Carpenter, indeed, entered the Dun, having forced the Timli Pass; but the little fort of Kalanga held out, and a grave disaster befell the British force by which it was besieged.

The Gurkha commandant defended the fort with a weak battalion, repelling three assaults, during which the brave Sir Rollo Gillespie was killed, together with a number of British officers and men far exceeding that of the little garrison; further eastward the British General conducted the campaign with the utmost imbecility, declaring his need of more guns and men. When reinforced, and with odds of ten to one, he still held back, at last mounting his horse by night and riding away, all alone, to his headquarters. These disgraceful events occurred, be it noted, in the year before Waterloo, while Arthur Wellesley was driving Soult over the Pyrenees.

In that hour of darkness a great leader appeared, in the person of General Ochterlony, afterwards so shamefully treated in the affair of Bhurtpur. While this good and gallant officer was advancing to the operations which ultimately had such a happy end, Gardner's accurate vision detected a weak place in the long line of the enemy by which he hoped to effect a most valuable co-operation.

The Gurkhas had been making annexations which became a cause of weakness rather than of strength; with an army of not much over 12,000 strong they had a frontier of about 700 miles to defend. About half-way between Katmandoo, their capital, and Malaon, their westernmost fortress, lay the beautiful sub-alpine Province of Kumaon, where the Government of the North-West Provinces has now its pleasant headquarters during the burning summer of Hindustan. On the north it is bounded by the finest *Oberland* in the world, with passes into Thibet, lower than the glacier-strewn peaks, but themselves higher than any of our European mountains; the rivers—which are numerous—flow east and south until they fall at last into the mighty Ganges below, and the valleys thus formed are the natural approaches to the country. On the dividing ridges are plateaux and fertile uplands, now covered with profitable woods or flourishing tea-plantations: on the crest of one of these was a Gurkha fort called Almora; but the garrison was weak. The newly-conquered races by which Kumaon was peopled were sparse and of gentle nature; the Gurkha troops were more required elsewhere; and Gardner, detecting with a soldier's eye the weakness and at the same time the value of the province, wrote to his cousin to propose its immediate occupation. On this the Resident at Dehli gave Edward orders to move upon the Dun—by this time cleared of the enemy—and a Captain Hearsey, whose name we recollect in the service of George Thomas, was sent on a reconnaisance in Kumaon.

On the 21st of November, 1814, Major Gardner wrote a somewhat doubtful letter to his cousin, to which he added an important postscript:

"It appears to me that your army (when you get it) will score as a false attack if we are otherwise successful. At all events, it will help to divide their force and distract them, while it will prevent reinforcements going to Amar Singh." That was the name of the Gurkha General against whom Ochterlony was then operating. "On mature consideration this is my idea."

It was the final decision of a resolute mind that only seemed to vacillate while both sides of the question had been under consideration. For the words just quoted contained a strategic conclusion in the way to immediate effect. The plan was adopted and proved the solution of the north-east frontier problem, not for the moment only, but for the remaining three-quarters of the nineteenth century.

A week later Edward was prepared to start for Kumaon, and the Major was with him. At the end of January, 1815, while Marley was fumbling on the eastern extremity and Ochterlony operating on the west, beyond Simla, the sub-alpine hills were invaded by a compact force of native infantry with some light guns. Hearsey was in a scrape, having been surprised by the enemy and carried a prisoner to Almora. But the ex-Minister of the Kumaoni Raja, whom the Gurkhas had dispossessed, was on the side of the invaders, and with his assistance the country became most friendly and the campaign prospered. On the 25th of April, 1815, Almora was attacked by Gardner at the head of his irregulars; the Gurkhas sallied out in defence, but were driven back. Reinforced by 2,000 regulars under Colonel—afterwards Sir Jasper—Nicolls, Gardner stormed the heights commanding the place, and effected an entry into the town. During the night he repulsed an energetic attempt of the enemy to disturb his possession, and on the following morning carried the fort by negotiation, preceded by a vigorous assault. The same evening Gardner was deputed to confer with the Gurkha commander; finally, the Gurkhas agreed to give up their strong places, let Hearsey go, and entirely evacuate the province. Gardner remained at Almora for some time with his levies, cutting off Amar Singh from his base; and that brave soldier, deprived of reinforcements, deserted by many of his followers, and constrained by his own officers, surrendered to Ochterlony on the 10th May, engaging to abandon all the Gurkha conquests west of the Jumna and to send orders for the evacuation of the rest of the hill-country up to the eastern border of Kumaon.

The full consequences of this were not immediately reaped, because Amar Singh, when he returned to headquarters, was compelled by his Government to break his agreement and try conclusions once more. On the 12th February of the succeeding year the indefatigable Ochterlony renewed the attack, striking this time at the enemy's capital. Peace was finally made on the 3rd March, 1816; and the gallant Gurkhas have, like the Sikhs, similarly subdued in later years, been amongst our best friends from the day of their submission. Of the particular value of Gardner's plan of campaign we have two indications. It facilitated the complete close of the war, and it gave to Upper India three or four *sanitaria* where business is transacted, health restored, and a reserve force of white troops maintained. The possession of such places as Simla and Naini Tal has its dangerous side, perhaps, to consider which is beyond our present scope. But the value, from a military point of view, of Landour, Ranikhet, and other convalescent depots for white troops can hardly be exaggerated.

In 1817 Gardner was rewarded by the incorporation of his corps with the cavalry of the Company's army, and it is still represented in the Indian Army List as the "2nd Bengal Cavalry." In 1824 he commanded it in Arakan, during the first Burmese War, with the local rank of Colonel and with high encomium from General Morrison, his immediate commanding-officer.

Gardner's warfare was accomplished, and the administration of his old commander made an end of the great Anarchy. Moira was created Marquess of Hastings, and finally fell into money trouble and died, in poverty and exile. But his work, too, was done; and in importance is more deserving of a place in history than that of men whose names are more generally remembered.[1]

Gardner spent the rest of his life as a country gentle-

[1] For a brief summary of this administration in its military and political aspects, see next chapter.

man, save for a short and uneventful campaign in Rajputāna. He commanded his old regiment—now the 2nd Bengal Cavalry—and in 1822 obtained the welcome distinction of being reinstated in the royal army with the rank of Lieutenant-Colonel, the commission bearing the date of his leaving Holkar—25th September, 1803. The wife of his youth continued to be dear to his advancing years, with one singular result, that all his offspring were married to natives of India, and their descendants have adopted the native life. The last Lord Gardner was his grandson; and of this nobleman Debrett affords the following description:—

"Alan Hyde, *born* July 1st, 1836; was sometime in a Native Police Force; described in marriage-certificate as 'a Trader': married March 12th, 1879, by a Methodist Minister in the house of his father to Jane (a native Indian), daughter of Angam Shekoh, and has issue living, Alan Legge, *born* October 25th, 1881. *Residence:* Village of Munowta, Nadri, Etah, N.-W.P., India." Lady Gardner is the grandchild of the last King of Dehli, in whom terminated the line of Timur, known as the "Great Moghal." This Eurasian nobleman died in 1899, leaving a son and heir (*vide* App. III.)

Whatever may be thought of a noble British race thus absorbed in Asiatic stagnation—like the Greeks of Menander—no one can question the merits of William Linnæus Gardner. He was a specimen of the British gentleman of a high type; handsome, tall, and brave; a good horseman and devoted to all kinds of sport. Partly educated in France, he possessed considerable European culture; history, blue-books, and even scientific works, all interested his mind; he was acquainted with mathematics; could survey and draw maps.

At last all these experiences and gifts came to a peaceful end: Colonel Gardner died, in his country house at Khāsganj, 29th July, 1835, and was soon followed in death by his faithful Begum. Nothing more need be said to show the inaccuracy of our great novelist's caricature. Like the fictitious "Gahagan," indeed, the deceased adventurer had bearded the truculent Holkar in Durbar, and won the affections of a princess. But, unlike the imagined swashbuckler, he was a modest, retiring gentleman, with strong rural proclivities and a hatred of self-assertion almost morbid.[1]

Skinner and Gardner are, further, noticeable as the founders of that admirable force which, first under the title of "Irregular Cavalry," and subsequently as "Bengal Cavalry," has become one of the most distinguished items of the British Army.

[1] We have seen that Gardner had served under Rawdon at Quiberon in 1795: when that nobleman, as Lord Moira, came up the country, in 1814, Gardner would not recall himself to the notice of the Governor-General, though urged to do so by friends. By a curious coincidence an adventurer of the same name appeared subsequently at the Court and camp of Ranjit Singh of Lahore (*vide Colonel Alexander Gardner*, etc., by Major Hugh Pearse; Edinburgh, 1898—a book of deep interest; but the two Gardners were not of kin, Alexander being an American of Scottish origin). For some interesting particulars relating to W. L. Gardner I have been indebted to a privately printed record kindly communicated by Major-General Renouard James, late Royal Engineers.

CHAPTER XV

Anarchy not quite closed by wars of 1803-4—Lords of Misrule—Earl of Moira appointed Governor-General—State of India in 1813—Moira's programme—Siege of Hathras—Pindari War—Comparison of British and native systems—A permanent catastrophe to be averted.

THE reign of chaos had fostered the operations of the foreign adventurers of whom W. L. Gardner was the last and the most useful. Some attempt to introduce order followed the wars of the beginning of the nineteenth century, with a somewhat uncertain and not very successful attitude of the British authorities, which came to be known as "non-intervention," and caused considerable mischief. The power of the East India Company—occasionally inspired and controlled by the King's Government—had battered some of the native Powers into helpless syncope, which left them an easy prey to their enemies and plunderers. By a conventional fiction the Moghal of Dehli was considered sovereign over the whole peninsula; but a number of local rulers—legitimate or usurping—held the practical sway in the various provinces. Some were descendants of ancient Hindu dynasties, like Travancore and Mysore in the South, and the Rājput chiefs in Mewar and Mārwar: others—of whom the most prominent were the Turkman House of Haidarabad and the Persian dynasty in Oudh—were representatives of Muslim officials who, in the decay of the Empire, had succeeded in erecting independent thrones; while a third group consisted of more recent aggregates made into States by Maratha leaders, such as the Peshwa at Poona, Sindhia and Holkar, and the Bhonsla of Berar.

But this unconnected mass of principalities was by no means an end of anarchy. The Nawabs and Rajas were, for the most part, Lords of Misrule, indifferent to the interests of their subjects, and mainly engaged in mutual hostility and rapine. So far as any constitutional theory remained, all were vassals or ministers of the Court at Dehli—even the British held most of their possessions under Imperial Patent—but in practice all exercised a kind of despotism, only mitigated by disorder or war.

Such was the confused and anomalous condition of Hindustan in 1813, ten years after the so-called "conquest." The Anarchy, begun in 1759 by the murder of the Emperor Alamgir II., had terminated, in theory, by the appearance of General Lake in the Durbar of that Emperor's son in September, 1803. But the valid authority needed to maintain peace and order had not as yet been established. In England the authority that was needed to foster and protect British interests in the East was not in a much more efficient or regular position. After the defeat of the premature attempt at reformation, introduced in 1783 by Burke and Fox, a modified application of parliamentary control had been brought about which led to the virtual subordination of political power formerly held by the Company, while the symbols of administration and the direction of a commercial monopoly remained untouched. Originated by Dundas in consultation with Lord Cornwallis, this policy was definitely laid down by the Declaratory Act of 1788, and confirmed by the renewed Charter of 1793. The views of Cornwallis were those of a high-minded statesman. He looked on the consultative voice left to the directors of the Company as a useful reality which quite justified the assumption that they were still the rulers of Indian affairs; not only did it seem that the policy to be pursued, but also that the choice of those by whom that policy was to be carried out, was in ordinary times to be based upon the views of the directors; while the monopoly of trade was deemed necessary to hinder the incursion of lawless adventurers.

By the time when these matters came up for fresh discussion, at the expiry of the Company's twenty years' lease, events had occurred which showed that some of the old machinery had been ill-devised, while other parts had fallen into obsolescence. Questions of importance had arisen in many directions, some due to increasing strength on one side, some to growing weakness on the other. Below all others, and a necessary element in their solution, was that regarding the nature of British authority in the Orient. With China, indeed, there need be, for the present, no difficulty. The Company sent their clippers and armed vessels to Canton, where they exchanged British produce for Chinese without risk or friction. The people of Canton were not pleasant to deal with, but they knew what they wanted, and had a certain system, once it was understood; and their Government, however backward, was not weak. But with Bengal transactions had not always allowed the same simplicity of action, while the surrounding Governments were ill-organised and faithless to an unusual degree. To carry on trade with such people demanded, for various reasons, the display of power, and the outgoing Governor, Lord Minto, had found it necessary to despatch an ambassador to more than one of his neighbours, and to assume, in so doing, the full attributes of sovereignty. In the case of Persia this position was hotly contested by the London Foreign Office, and at one moment there were two rival British envoys at Teheran, one representing the Governor-General and one the King of England. Minto defended himself stoutly, asserting that the Company's Government was vested with sovereignty within its own boundaries and that its claims had been admitted by the Shah. "This acknowledged character," so he argued, "as it constituted the basis, so it must form the cement, of our external relations." What sort of fabric it could be which admitted of the same substance for mortar and foundation was not distinctly shown, but the assertion was of a kind that could hardly fail to be taken up by the Ministry in London, and probably contributed to the fall of the bold Viceroy. The question of sovereignty was seen to involve two others. If the Company were a sovereign, ought sovereigns to trade? If the Company were a trader, ought it to be invested with sovereign power?

The commercial element was felt to be fundamental. The Company had been established for trade purposes, and in the course of years had acquired political power for the maintenance of commerce. In 1813 the British Islands produced most of their own food, but a great and growing demand for Oriental luxuries had sprung up, while the rapidly developing manufacturing interest was dependent on Eastern sources for much of its raw matter. Long ago had Adam Smith observed upon the singularity of the attempt "to found a great Empire for the sole purpose of raising up a people of customers"; but since his time the attempt had come into the sphere of practical politics—the British nation had dimly perceived the advantage of a permanent connection with an enormous population which should take British fabrics and pay for them in raw material. In the beginning, indeed, it had not been so simple, and the imports from India had consisted largely of muslins and longcloths; but, by the time of which we are now thinking, a vast production of cheap piece-goods had begun in England, so that the value of Indian textiles imported into the country had fallen from three millions sterling to a few thousand pounds, while the trade was so disorganised that the Company had to call home the cash balances held in reserve in India. When the question of renewing the Charter came to be dealt with, grave doubts began to be expressed as to the use of the Company's commercial monopoly, and many seemed to think that if that monopoly were ended the semblance of sovereignty might end also. The President of the Board of Control was of opinion that the objects of the Company's privilege had ceased to exist, save, perhaps, for the purpose of bringing tea from China and carrying thither in exchange the broadcloths of Yorkshire and the opium of Bengal. In China, indeed, the Company was solely engaged by these commercial occupations, having no territorial possessions, and being freed by the comparative strength and unity of the native Government from all political complications. But in the case of India political relations were essential to trade, and the two questions were closely intertwined, so that the struggle which began in April, 1812, was a somewhat perplexed affair, alike in Parliament and in the country. The bias of public opinion was in favour of the maintenance of the Company as a governing body invested with patronage, a power which no one seemed disposed to entrust to a partisan Cabinet. On the side of trade much discontent doubtless existed at "the outports," as the provincial seats of maritime commerce were called; but the influence of Bristol and Liverpool was not much greater at that period than the influence of Bodmin or Grampound, and the power of the Company was energetically put forth to controvert their pleadings.

While Parliament was dealing with the claims of the East India Company in England, an elderly military man was carelessly sent to India to mould the destiny of countless millions in that remote region and establish the power of the Crown. Moira's early life—as already noticed in connection with Gardner—had given little indication of future greatness or preparation for the higher duties of statesmanship. As Colonel Rawdon he had served with some distinction, and ultimately been employed as Adjutant-General of the army engaged in the vain attempt to subdue the Americans and their French allies. On his return to Europe he was created Baron Rawdon in the Irish peerage, and afterwards succeeded his father as second Earl of Moira. In 1795 he once more assisted at a British defeat, having been sent with a small detachment in aid of Sombreuil's attempt at Quiberon, on the shore of Brittany, which was so easily repulsed by the Republican army under Hoche.[1] For the next few years Moira led the life of a Member of the House of Commons and man of fashion, professing the politics of Fox, and associated intimately with the Prince of Wales. In 1806 he was rewarded by the post of Master-General of the Ordnance; and, on the Prince becoming Regent, was enabled to take a small part in political affairs. In May, 1812, the Tory Prime Minister was shot in the Lobby of the House, and the Prince entered upon negotiations with some of the Whig leaders with the object of strengthening the Cabinet by the admission of Liberal statesmen favoured by the Commons. Into the details of these transactions it is not necessary to enter here; suffice it to note that Moira, as a Whig and old acquaintance, was employed to endeavour the conciliation of the Marquess Wellesley. A tangled controversy followed; Moira's political efforts were finally defeated, mainly by the insincerity of the Prince, who formed a Ministry of somewhat obsolete character and threw Moira overboard. There being no vacant post with which the negotiating Earl could be decorously compensated, the Court of Directors was ordered to recall Minto and appoint Moira Governor-General of India in his place.

The modern Viceroy has a post of honour and of labour, and the salary—the nominal amount of which has not been increased for over one hundred years—is

[1] This was the occasion on which W. L. Gardner first served under the future Governor-General.

no longer the temptation that it once was. But he leads a pleasant life, having a charming summer residence in a lovely mountain retreat, with the full prestige of representing the British Crown, and provided with a splendid personal staff, and with a luxurious railway-carriage ready to convey him to his Calcutta palace in the winter or to waft him about among peaceful landscapes and old historic cities. He is always in the prime of life, assisted by councillors who act as his Ministers in different departments, and relieve him of all responsibility in administrative details. In military affairs he is aided by the experienced officer who commands the Indian forces. Far different was the case of Moira: a man verging on his twelfth lustre; charged with the double duty of civil ruler and Commander-in-Chief; encumbered by the aid of civilian experts in Council—men of strong opinions and characters. His headquarters in Calcutta were hot and unwholesome; if he wished to see into things for himself, he was confined to the alternative of following the course of the Ganges in a houseboat or wandering over a roadless wilderness with tents and baggage and a crowd of followers who devastated the land. His position was, at this moment, further embarrassed by a total uncertainty as to the fate of the Company whose servant he ostensibly was; and the support of the feeble Cabinet was not to be assumed by a man opposed to them in politics and recently engaged in efforts to keep them out of office.

Thus handicapped, Moira undertook the perilous adventure: unversed in the practice of governing, but possessed of a resolute and intelligent mind. Like any wise man approaching such a task, he must have known that great difficulties awaited him; and, indeed, his private journal is enough to show that he was not only aware of those difficulties, but was earnestly preparing to deal with them.[1] The southern part of India was in no

[1] *Private Journals of the Marquess of Hastings*, 2 vols., 1858.

very unsettled condition, save in so far as it included a portion of the territories subject to the Maratha Peshwa. In the Telugu and Tamil districts Munro was introducing prosperity and order; financial scandal was brewing in the Deccan, but its full fermentation was yet to come. Nearer the Narbada river, however, the marauding bands of the Pindaris were extending the limits of desolation under protection and abetment of the contiguous Maratha States, while Upper India was divided between robber-barons and disbanded soldiers, the dregs of former war. The average Indian citizen, whose craving was, as it always is, for peace and protection, groaned audibly; and a man accustomed to ideas of duty and discipline could not be deaf to such complaints. In the first volume of his *Journals* he relates how, at his tour in 1814, a respectable agriculturist of Oudh asked a British officer, "When are you going to take this wretched country?"

But peace, as is usual, was to be purchased; the price was—War: and that war might have to invoke support from the energies and authority of the mother-country. Without indulging himself with the contemptuous language of Lord Wellesley towards "the cheesemongers of Leadenhall Street," Moira's sincerity of vision showed him that the ultimately responsible power was that of the Crown and Parliament of England; and he observed within six months of his accession that his object ought to be "to render the British Government paramount, in effect if not declaredly" (*Journals*, vol. i., 1814).

In the days of the Regency there was a frontier trouble not very dissimilar to that of recent times, though in a different direction. The peninsula of India has been called the Italy of Asia, and, if Cabul and the Vaziri hills can be regarded as its Piédmont, the Tyrol may be taken as represented by Nepal. Here, on the boundary of the great Chinese Empire and under its remote vassalage, was a mountain land occupied by hardy races, of which the most famous and predominant was the *Gurkha*, a mixed breed of Mongolian and Hindu who had absorbed the adjacent hills and were encroaching on the plains below. What with these Gurkha incursions and the lawlessness in Central India, the Governor-General foresaw "the elements of a war more general than any that we have hitherto encountered" (*Journals*, vol. i. p. 47). But he did not shrink from the danger. After vain attempts at negotiation, thwarted by the ignorant audacity of the mountaineers, he addressed an ultimatum to the Gurkha Durbar, and, on meeting a prompt and insolent defiance, sent four divisions of troops to operate on so many portions of the frontier—some seven hundred miles in length. Into the at first disastrous details of this war we have already thrown a passing look: one General was shot in trying to storm a fort with cavalry; another lost his head so completely as to mount his horse by night and desert his command. We have also seen how, with valuable help from Major Gardner, the Nepalese line of defence was cut in two. The final campaign was entrusted to the more competent hands of Ochterlony, who routed the brave enemy successively at both extremities of the line; and the Durbar, after a futile call for Chinese help, finally capitulated and entered into an alliance with the British Government, which has subsisted ever since.

But the chief immediate result was to show Moira that it was necessary for him to assume his place as Commander-in-Chief the next time he went to war. In the Indian armies he could find no General of the necessary ability excepting Ochterlony, who was wanted for the delicate duties of his permanent appointment as Resident at the Court of Dehli. When, therefore, in 1816 the condition of Central India became intolerable, Moira deemed it his duty to take the field in person. Not that he could divest himself in the least degree of his administrative work. Seldom has a Proconsul been in a more trying situation. Of the Council bequeathed to him by Minto, the strongest members were opposed to his policy, which was, moreover, discountenanced, and even prohibited, by the authorities at home, while at the same time the pressure of internal trouble was going on side by side with the anxieties of the military operations. In 1815 disturbances occurring in Cutch and Katiawar—outlying provinces of Gujarat—were suppressed, without loss of life, by Colonel East. In the following year a riot, which nearly assumed the importance of actual rebellion, broke out at Bareilly, in the neighbourhood of the small Rohila State of Rampur, serious opposition to a new house-tax being made use of as a pretext by Muslim disaffection. Supported by the presence of Afghan adventurers at Rampur and by the collusive absence of the Nawab of that little principality, the Mohammedans of Bareilly committed great excesses, murdering an inoffensive young Englishman and twice resisting the police; nor did the tumult subside until a number, estimated at 1,500, had been killed or wounded. A still more serious affair occurred on the other side of the Ganges, where the robber-barons, who had been mostly reduced to order by Lake, were still represented by the powerful Talukdars of Mursan and Hathras. These two tracts, which to-day are crossed by railways and noted only for their fertile soil and their industrious population, were then controlled by lawless landlords, of Jat families, the chief being Daya Ram, whose headquarters were at Hathras town. Here, in the weakness of a new administration, he had been allowed to erect a castle fortified in imitation of the adjacent British fort of Aligurh. In 1817, fourteen years after Lake had put down the Maratha power by what was officially taken to be "conquest," the Government determined to dismantle Daya Ram's stronghold, and enforced the order by a division of the Bengal Army under Major-General Dyson Marshall. Six cavalry regiments, two battalions of British infantry, seven of sepoys, with seventy-one mortars and howitzers and thirty-four siege-guns, formed part of an expedition on a scale which showed that Moira meant no trifling. The town was speedily breached and stormed, but the contumacious Jat still held his citadel. It was accordingly bombarded continuously for fifteen hours, in the course of which the powder-magazine was exploded with terrible loss of life. The rebel chief with a few followers, all in full armour, issued from a sally-port and cut his way through the Bengal Cavalry, a gallant feat which was ultimately followed by his capture and pardon. The country submitted, though the fact that the submission did not happen till the fourteenth year after Lake's victorious campaign is an instance of tardy pacification after a seeming conquest. An insurrection, yet more grave than that of Bareilly, next ensued in Orissa, where general distress had been produced by fiscal errors, and had found leaders in a body of public servants hurriedly disestablished. In 1817 the "Paiks," as these superfluous employees were called, broke out under the instigation of an official of a local Raj, who had been also affected by reduction of expense. Two detachments of troops sent against them were repulsed, and a European officer was killed. The sacred town of Jagannath was occupied by the insurgents, and the commanding officer retired with his men. The whole district of Puri now rose in arms, but the Raja held aloof, and the movement collapsed after one action, in which the rebels were routed by Colonel Le Fèvre with one sepoy battalion. The Government acted with commendable promptitude in relief of the grievances thus indicated. A special commission being appointed to hold a local inquiry, what was found wrong was righted, and the district has ever since been orderly and peaceful, in spite of its being the scene of pilgrimages, in the course of which it is often thronged by hundreds of thousands of fanatical Hindus in their most fanatical condition.

So far, therefore, the Governor-General had prospered in all his undertakings. But a weighty charge was still upon him if peace and order were to be permanently provided for the people of India. At the beginning of Moira's rule the British Government was not directly answerable for more than Bengal, the North-West Provinces, the Carnatic, and a narrow strip of the western coast, with the Heptanesia of Bombay, to which were now added the acquisitions arising out of the treaty with Nepal, little more than the sub-Himalaya country from Naini Tal to Simla. With these exceptions, India was under native sway, including Oudh, the Punjab, Rajputāna, the Deccan, and Mysore—each equal to a first-class European kingdom in area and resources. But this disproportion was to be construed by the light of Lord Moira's peculiar view. We have seen what this was: after his first discussion with a Council imbued with the "non-intervention" policy of an earlier period, Moira had recorded that he meant to make the British power "paramount in effect, if not declaredly so"; while he saw the concurrent danger—so often pointed out by Munro—of degrading the Princes and their subjects, implied by domineering interference. He deplored the "captious bickerings" which were constantly coming to his notice, and considered that "a rational jealousy of our power was not likely to excite half the intrigues against us which must naturally be produced by the wanton provocations which we have been giving on trivial subjects to all the States around." Seeds of hostility had thus been sown, which would germinate on favourable opportunity. No sooner would the British power be seriously involved than all who had a grudge to wreak would endeavour to combine in active aggression. In short, the task undertaken by Lord Moira was to make every Raja and Nawab govern with humanity and efficiency under the general supervision and control of the civilised power, which did not wish to coerce any of them, and yet acknowledged the responsibility of superior strength and wisdom. And if that task should lead to resistance, he was prepared to meet resistance and to put it down.

That the spirit of some of the native Durbars was bad, Moira was certified by his Agents, R. Jenkins, at the Court of the Bhonsla, and Mountstuart Elphinstone at Poona ; for these were intrepid men, never likely to give undue alarms. For active operations he was doubly unprepared ; the finances were drained by recent remittances to London, and action was positively prohibited by the India House and by the Regent's Government : the policy of the Ministry, in fact, was conveyed through the channel of the "Secret Committee" of the East India Company ; and the Governor-General—so long as his Council refused support—was not in a position to fly in the face of authority.

Luckily, the audacity of the Pindaris at length produced the acquiescence of the Bengal Council, and Moira, ably backed by Mr. C. (afterwards Lord) Metcalfe, resolved on attacking the marauders, even though the doing so brought on him the resistance of the Maratha chiefs and the censure of the Board of Control. In neglecting the cautions and even positive prohibitions from London, Moira was probably guided by his knowledge of the character of the men with whom he had to deal. It was in vain that men of the school of Perceval and Liverpool denied that there was any serious movement going on in Central India, when the Pindaris themselves were ever ready to supply an *Eppur si muove.* In Minto's time they had already ventured on transgressing the boundaries of British India and carrying fire and sword into the District of Mirzapur ; and since that time they had been harassing the borders and making raids into the Deccan, long continued impunity being the source of increasing boldness. In 1814 the disbanded soldiers and indigenous brigands had amalgamated with a solidarity independent of caste or creed, one company calling itself after Sindhia and the other invoking the name of Holkar; with a few guns and a small force of infantry, but mainly consisting of predatory horsemen armed with lances and carrying on their saddle-bows all that they required excepting the bare flour and water which they could reckon upon finding in the villages that they harried, or the quarters of the Rajas by whom they were harboured. They were favoured, and to some extent supported, by Amir Khan, a retired partisan leader who had once given sore trouble to Lake; their immediate leaders being two degenerated Muslim and a Jat named Chitu, the ablest of the whole, who had been assigned five Districts in what are now known as the "Central Provinces." Up to 1814, however, the Home Government was busy with the Peninsular War; and the fact that the marauders were notoriously abetted by many powerful Native States increased rather than otherwise the reluctance felt by mediocre men to acknowledge responsibility for action. To restore order in Central India, so it was argued, would be to incur Sindhia's hostility and finally involve oneself in a general war with the entire Maratha confederacy. Inspired by Metcalfe, the Governor-General held that this was not a certain consequence, and that, even if it were certain, it ought to be encountered, the honour and even the safety of the Government being at stake. The Council differed, and the case was sent home for fresh consideration; but the mail had hardly left Calcutta when the growing audacity of the Pindaris precipitated the solution. Suddenly darting into the Northern Sirkars, they held a ten days' orgy of rapine and ruin, in which nearly two hundred British subjects were killed and many thousands tortured and robbed, while respectable married women escaped dishonour only by leaping into wells. According to official reports, the total loss of property was equivalent to a million sterling, and the number of the marauders was estimated at 23,000. Almost at the same time arrived fresh instructions from London prohibiting offensive operations; but the Council was at last learning to realise that the time for action had arrived, and that the orders had been issued upon a state of things that had ceased to exist. A change, too, occurred at home, where the Earl of Buckinghamshire died and was succeeded at the Board of Control by George Canning; while the general peace which prevailed after the removal from the scene of the Emperor Napoleon set free the moral and other energies of the British nation.

In December, 1816, as we learn from an entry of the 23rd in the *Private Journal*, the last hesitation had been overcome, and the Council was "ready to record an unanimous opinion that the extirpation of the Pindarries (*sic*) must be undertaken notwithstanding the orders of the Court of Directors." The Governor-General could, indeed, do nothing—he adds—so long as the Councillors, appealing to orders from home, could clog his action with adverse minutes; but now he felt free to act according to his own views. Fortunately a change of spirit at home followed on Canning's accession to office, and, even before the change had occurred in the views of the Calcutta Council, new instructions had been already dictated to the Secret Committee, in which Moira was informed that his proposed measures would now be approved, even if they should extend beyond repelling invasion to the work of "pursuing and chastising the invaders." And if Sindhia or any other chief should take part with the Pindaris, such chief should be treated as an enemy.

By the time that this despatch could arrive in India the Government there had become committed to somewhat stronger action. Amir Khan was intimidated into total quiescence—he was growing old and rich; Sindhia's isolation was ensured by a firm ultimatum, backed by a cordon of British troops, and vigorous measures were adopted towards the Bhonsla and the Peshwa. Large bodies of men, under the best Generals available, began to converge on Central India; and on July 5, 1817, the Governor-General left Calcutta to assume the general direction of military and political operations in that region.

These were completely successful. The Bhonsla broke into open hostility, only to be deposed; the Peshwa attacked the Residency at Poona, where he was defeated and put to flight; the Pindaris were dispersed or hunted down, Chitu being devoured by a tiger while lurking in his native jungle. The native dynasty was restored in the Bhonsla dominions, in the person of a minor, in whose name Mr. Jenkins ruled the administration. At Poona the *gadi* of the faithless Peshwa was declared vacant and his post abolished; but the smaller Maratha States were preserved and made more efficient. The old principalities of Rajputāna, freed at last from plunder and anarchy, resumed their autonomy. In the well-chosen words of a profound and original thinker:

"Henceforward it became the universal principle of public policy that every State in India should make over the control of its foreign relations to the British Government, should submit all external disputes to British arbitration, and should defer to British advice regarding internal management, so far as might be necessary to cure disorder or serious misrule. This political settlement established universal recognition of the cardinal principle upon which the fabric of British dominion in India has been built up" (Sir A. Lyall, *Rise of British Dominion in India*, ch. xvi.).

The Governor-General, after this vast group of successes due to his own courage and skill, received the barren honour of a step in the peerage, and retired (after an unhappy scandal at Haidarabad) to die, as Marquess of Hastings, in poverty and exile. But what alone concerns us here is to note the great outline of his policy and the mischief that ensued upon its abandonment by his successors. The ideal of Lord Hastings had been Oriental administration under English control, the utmost independence of Native Powers that could be made compatible with the demands of common humanity. In later days another policy prevailed; no opportunity was to be lost for introducing direct European action (Dalhousie); in ruling Asiatics we were to be guided, not by their conscience, but by our own (John Lawrence).

The two subjects of sanitation and education may be regarded as instances of difficulty due to the forcible introduction of the ideals of one state of society into the affairs of another. The hygienic system of the British nation has by no means eliminated all classes of epidemic disease, but it may claim to have prolonged life and increased the numbers of the census. But in India conditions are totally diverse: you have a non-emigrating rural population already pressing dangerously on the means of subsistence in good seasons, and in times of scarcity afflicted with hopeless suffering; you have not either the money or the men to enforce efficient sanitary practice on the villages, or even on your own cantonments, and the imperfect measures of sanitation that can alone be effected often do more harm than good. An excellent and most loyal Indian newspaper not long ago published figures proving that in a number of conspicuous municipalities the death-rate had risen from thirty to thirty-two since the attempts to sanitate had been completed. As for "education"—so-called—it is to be observed that primary instruction is provided by the law, but is optional; that secondary instruction is in a most incomplete state; and that the results of the Colleges and Universities are to be found in the existence of a large and growing body of discontented "Baboos," who eke out an income by maintaining litigation or levying blackmail by means of a licentious and unnecessary journalism.[1]

Now, here are matters on which the British rulers of India have long prided themselves, and which can be brought to the test of fact. Judged by that irrefragable evidence, what do we find ? An increase in the normal death-rate, an uncontrollable prevalence of the most deadly epidemics, occasional devastations of famine, sanguinary wars on the frontier, abuse of free speech and printing within the borders of the Empire, and a revenue that barely meets the daily needs and leaves no balance for sinking-fund or insurance, so that the national debt increases year by year, while the credit of the Government slowly declines.

We must always admit that Dalhousie and Lawrence were good and able men ; yet we may have to conclude that the gifts of civilisation conferred on India by them were not unadulterated. Population has increased, but so has care : "Thou hast multiplied the nation, but not increased the joy." Commerce has developed, but the wage of inland labour does not rise in proportion. The country in the last few years has suffered all the calamities from which we pray to be delivered. The fact is that India still endures the standards of the early Victorian age, which were those of persons for whom sewage and the three R's possessed a sort of millennial sanctity. To a House of Commons elected by the middle-classes these things appeared "a mission," and the easy-going ways of the Regency were, no doubt, somewhat shocking; but it is not quite certain that the early Victorian Reformers introduced any great improvement into the condition of India. Lord Hastings, one must admit, extended direct British administration to a very considerable region—to some of what are now known as the Central Provinces, and to the greater part of the present

[1] This is not meant to apply to the many Indian papers of good repute.

Bombay Presidency, as apart from Sindh. He could not well do otherwise; the imbecility and faithlessness of the Maratha chiefs probably left him but little choice. Nevertheless, it will be observed that his annexations originated altogether in the Pindari War, which he undertook both against advice in India and against orders from London, and at the risk of his life and reputation. He felt indignant at the supineness which would have left the British boundaries exposed to trespass by murderous marauders, and he sacrificed his own ease and comfort, at an advanced age, that he might do what he conceived his duty. But he attempted no more: in spite of provocation, he spared Sindhia and the Gaikwar; he even tried to spare the faithless Appa Sahib, and maintained the Bhonsla dynasty at Nāgpur. The ancient dynasty of Satára was restored; the feeble Rājput States were respected and strengthened; and nothing was done that had the least appearance of introducing English administration on doctrinary grounds, Nāgpur itself being only undertaken temporarily and in the interest of the Bhonsla House. With the Gurkhas of Nepal was concluded an enduring peace, taking, however, no territory but what had previously belonged to Bengal, in addition to a small and barren stretch of mountain in which the Nepalese themselves were intruders, and where, so far as they could be found, the original owners were also restored, the Rajas of Tehri and the like.

Far different is the India to which we are introduced by modern publicists. But even here a third of the vast area is still administered by native rulers, with a population equal to that of modern Germany added to that of France. In some of these provinces the administration is aided or controlled by British advisers, as is the case with Egypt; in all the maintenance of certain general principles of humanity and justice is provided by the care of the paramount Power, grave derelictions being punished by deposition and the substitution of a better ruler. Peace and order are insured, and the States are protected from outward attack and debarred from war with one another. Thus a partial return to Moira's moderate policy has been made, and the two contrasted systems work side by side, at the same time, and almost in the same place.

It might be difficult to devise criteria by which the relative success of the methods could be tested. In the two-thirds of India which are directly governed, the rules of civilised polity are as rigorously enforced as in any country in the world, save only as regards civil law, which in most respects follows the religious codes of Hinduism or of Islam, as the case may be. A disputed succession in a Muslim family, a question of partition among Rājput brethren, will be decided by British Courts, according to the respective systems accepted by the parties; in the rare cases of litigation between a Hindu on one side and a Musalman on the other the code of the defendant will be applied. But in all cases of agrarian controversy, as in all criminal charges, enactments of the British Government must decide; and in the absence of a law of torts these cases are necessarily the major part of litigation. In regard to the collection of revenue, as in regard to the execution of decrees, an inflexible punctuality prevails, and is enforced —where such is required—by the exercise of sovereign power and the sanction of Imperial arms. In the so-called "Native States" all is different. A capricious exercise of authority, sometimes mild, often uncertain, is substituted for the systematic and mechanical rigour of European civilisation; a small *douceur* to a policeman may save a possible fine to the magistrate; and the lawless oppression of the great occasionally vexes the weaker classes, as was the case in England when the *Paston Letters* were written. All this used to appear—often yet appears—barbarous and even shocking; but it co-exists with a sort of gipsy freedom and absence of misunderstood regularity, which tempers it, and perhaps endears, to the Oriental mind. The superior population-rate of British India may be cited as a mark of superior administration ; on the other hand, the low rate in Native States is at least a cause of less competition. The chiefs and rulers may be less conscientious than British officials selected by the Civil Service Commission, but at least they possess the sympathies born of local feeling and local knowledge. And the career open to ambition, which gives to public life the excitement of a lottery, may seem barbarous to us and yet have its attractions for the people.

It is not pretended that any of these considerations, or even all of them together, should be accepted as a basis for exalting Oriental ways above those of the West, which would be the merest pedantry of paradox. But what is suggested is that methods and institutions based on Oriental tradition and custom may, if duly handled, prove more useful to an Eastern people than those arising out of an evolution to which such people are strangers. This *à priori* doctrine is, in fact, allowed in the sphere of law ; we do not try suits according to the *Koran* or the *Shaster* because we approve of those codes, but because they are more native to the men before us than Shelley's case or the Pandects. This was not always seen ; a learned Judge in Calcutta laid down, not so very long ago, that when the British first acquired Bengal there was a kind of legal vacuum, into which Grimgribber—to use Bentham's word—rushed as by force of Nature : for which, however, his lordship might have to go back for a precedent to the days of Hyde and Impey. It is related of those luminaries that, on landing (in 1774), they were scandalised by the bare legs of the men who carried their palanquins from the ghât : "Ah ! brother," cried one to the other, "the Supreme Court will have failed if ere long each of these honest fellows has not a pair of stockings to wear." That *obiter dictum* of the first judges was but a forecast of the view of their successor above cited.

But the Oriental methods must be duly handled: that proviso has been already made, to anticipate the scorn with which the friends of civilisation would naturally encounter a proposition not so guarded. The King, or Cadi, of Orientalism, sitting in the gate of his palace and deciding differences by the light of his own wit and conscience, has been suppressed in India, and his place taken by a trained Judge administering scientific codes of law. And why cannot the like be done in other departments? It is obviously right that the general requirements of humanity and good order should be met in any place where flags of Christian nations fly: but it is not so clear that such provision can never be made without the presence of large staffs of European functionaries, with the concomitant salaries, furlough allowances, and retiring pensions of the Indian Civil Service. If the uninformed philanthropy of the British voter insists on having in every village a Board School and a sanitary officer, the British Parliament will have to find the ways and means for such luxuries, in the long run. The Indian revenues cannot provide them; nor is it possible to run an Occidental administration upon an Oriental budget.

Nothing can be more unfair than the assertion of some of our would-be reformers to the effect that the people of India are suffering under a crushing weight of taxes. That is, indeed, the exact reverse of what is happening; and it is the difficulty of taxing such a population that forms the preliminary—and insurmountable—objection to forcing upon them an exotic civilisation, if that were otherwise shown to be right and proper. A revenue that is collected in copper[1] is called

[1] On the assumption that the whole of the taxation is paid by the inhabitants of British India, the payment per head—inclusive of provincial rates—falls at Rs. 1-4 (say 1s. 8d.) p.a. But in fact few of these taxes are obligatory, and the yearly incidence on the ordinary Indian is only about 7½d.

upon to maintain up-to-date institutions of war and peace; and the inevitable result is tending to make of British rule in India a permanent catastrophe, unless means can be devised for fully combining native sentiment with European method. It has been shown by Captain Mahan, U.S.A., that what Asia needs from Europe is not direct action, but influence.

CHAPTER XVI

India never self-governed—The Moghal Empire—Stages of a great Indian city—True nature of British "conquest"—Policy of Lord Wellesley—Russian appreciation—Bravery of natives and need of efficient leading.

BOTH sides of the shield have now been impartially considered: we have seen what are the drawbacks of civilisation, and what the cautions with which it ought to be introduced into countries long inured to Anarchy. The facts adduced in the above chapters convey lessons to the British nation as well as to the peoples of India. To the latter, at least, they would be useful as a reminder of the benefits that they have received from the assumption of Indian administration by a Western race. There is, no doubt, a certain element of hardness involved in the idea of conquest; and there have not been wanting among us, from the days of Edmund Burke to now, good men whose sympathies are excited when they think of vast and storied regions, whose inhabitants are deprived of independence and exposed to a sort of compulsory education. But well-informed Hindus could answer them, if they reflected on the condition in which their forefathers existed only a few generations ago, and on the prospects awaiting their descendants if the British were to leave the country.

So far as we like to look back, we discern no signs of autonomy in India, only vicissitudes of more or less selfish despotism, often exercised by foreigners in one part or another. The Anarchy that ensued after the taking of Dehli by the Persians, in 1738, might bear the name of

Home Rule if it had been "Rule" at all; if it had not made life a burden to the many and a deadly snare to the few. Moreover, long prior to that the country was under alien domination; and even the great Akbar favoured his own race, the Moghals, in the public service, and professed to take one-third of the gross produce of the land from the people; seeing that one-tenth has been almost universally recognised as the ideal ratio, we can see how oppressive was this famous revenue system, with all its efficiency and benevolent intentions. The successors of Akbar had Indian blood; yet under them the decay and decomposition of the Empire never stopped. In 1738 Nadir and his Persians almost bled the country to death under the feeble Mohammed Shah. At the death of that Emperor began the anarchy; "after his demise," writes a native historian, "everything went to wreck." The country soon became a scene that could hardly bear comparison with France after the Hundred Years' War. A native authority cited in Dow's *History of Hindustan* (published 1770) speaks of "every kind of social confusion. Villainy was practised in all its forms; law and religion were trodden under foot; the bonds of private friendship and connection, as well as society and government, were broken; and every individual—as if in a forest of wild beasts—could rely upon nothing but the strength of his own arm." A Persian traveller, Mohammed Hazin, had the fortune to go through the siege of Ispahan and the Afghan conquest of his country before coming to settle in India; and he thought his own country, under all sufferings, a better place of abode than Hindustan. "No man," he writes, "will ever stay in India of his own choice . . . unless he be one who unexpectedly arrives at wealth and distinction, and from lack of moral strength . . . becomes tranquil there and habituates himself to the life."

Is it necessary to multiply citations? We have seen what was the condition of the people under the best circumstances, in regions ruled by strong and fairly enlightened persons, such as the Begum and General Perron; and have found that the chief elements were oppression, exaction, maladministration of all sorts. Nor does this description apply only to the war-worn regions of the North. Reading of the twenty years following on the rise of Haidar in Mysore, we learn that the Marathas, occupied with constant forays, were inattentive to the misery of the people, whom their Governors "oppressed in the most cruel manner . . . neither the property nor the life of a subject can be called his own." Fuller details are to be found in the last chapter of *The Fall of the Moghal Empire*, a book by the present writer, chiefly taken from documents of the time. This evidence, it is true, relates chiefly to rural districts—but the life of the people was (and even yet continues to be) chiefly rural. The state of the towns may be imagined from the account of one of the great Moghal capitals given by a traveller who visited Lahore so late as 1809:—

"24th May.—I visited the ruins of Lahore, which afforded a melancholy picture of fallen splendour. Here the lofty dwellings and mosques which, fifty years ago, raised their tops to the skies, and were the pride of a busy and active population, are now crumbling into dust, and, in less than half a century more, will be levelled to the ground. In going over these ruins I saw not a human being—all was silence, solitude, and gloom."

In 1641 an earlier traveller had written of the same city that, "large as it appeared, there were not houses enough for the people, who were encamped for half a league outside. It is handsome and well-ordered. . . . I entered the city; a very difficult undertaking on account of the number of people who filled the streets . . . it is ornamented by fine palaces and gardens."

Thus low had the second city of the Empire fallen in

less than two centuries of persistent misgovernment. Yet in little more than the fifty years postulated for her total disappearance Lahore had renewed her youth. In 1865 the population had risen to 120,000 and was increasing at the rate of 1 per cent. yearly. The old monuments have now been preserved and restored; among recent buildings are found those of the Punjab University, the Oriental College, the State College, the Medical School, the Law School, the Normal School, the Mayo Hospital, the Museum, the Town Hall, and many other useful and sometimes ornamental structures : some of them erected, wholly or in great part, by the enterprise and munificence of native Princes and capitalists.

We hear sometimes of the unsympathetic attitude of the modern Rulers of India, as if they were mere conquerors eager to fill their own pockets. But in regard to this superficial view we must remember that, if the British were conquerors, it would be contrary to the experience of history that they should be quite sympathetic with the conquered. As it happens, India is not a conquered country, and has never been treated as such by the British. In a strictly legal sense, perhaps, a distinction had to be drawn between "ceded" and "conquered" provinces, in Upper India, because one portion had been acquired by treaty after war and the other by amicable arrangement : the Lower Duāb having been obtained, for a consideration, from the Nawab of Oudh, while the country from Cawnpore to Kurnal was extorted from Perron and his master.[1] Moira, too—as has been shown—overthrew the Peshwa and the Pindaris, but never made war upon the people.

Indeed, in the popular acceptation of the word, there was no conquest in either case, Sindhia and Perron being alike foreign intruders, whose own dominion there was

[1] This truth is treated with a masterly hand in Seeley's *Expansion of England*, where it is shown that, at the time of the so-called "conquest," India as a nation did not exist.

not of twenty-five years' date: while the Peshwa himself was but a usurper. By "conquest" is understood the bearing down by invasion of a more or less earnest national resistance; not merely the overthrow of unconstitutional rulers. In that case, where the people have opposed the invaders, they become—when the war is ended by their defeat—a subjugated body of persons liable to death, captivity, or enslavement. It has been laid down by international publicists that "the English system" is always imposed upon nations thus reduced to impotence by conquest; and a well-known writer on the matter cites the case of Ireland as affording a familiar illustration.

Now, from this point of view, it is clear that the Upper Provinces of India were never conquered: when Lake advanced from the "Ceded Provinces," the further part of the Duāb fell before his arms, so far as the defence of Perron and Sindhia was concerned. But Sindhia and Perron were, as already pointed out, foreign intruders themselves; and the real sovereign was the aged Emperor, who made no opposition, but, on the contrary, welcomed the British General and conferred upon him the second highest title in the old Moghal hierarchy. Neither did the people offer any resistance, nor any of their ancient Rajas or other dynasties; though certain robber-barons attempted sporadic insurrections and dacoities, as was naturally to be expected. This being so, the indigenous laws and customs were observed and maintained from that day to this, certain indispensable reforms excepted, which have been gradually introduced from time to time. To these there has been no great or general opposition; and, even in the temporary paralysis of power that followed on the Revolt of 1857, the bulk of the population held aloof from the mutineers and quickly returned to peaceful avocations as soon as the mutineers had been dispersed. The British Power resumed its operations—those of a schoolmaster rather than of a conqueror, the people going on, as of old, with their time-honoured opinions and practices; in every conceivable respect differing from the Gaels of Ireland, whose lands have been parted out amongst Anglo-Norman adventurers; their tribal system superseded by that known to us as "feudal"; their Brehon Law abolished to make way for the Common and Statute Law of the conquerors; their very language all but rooted out.

From this it will be seen why India is not, properly speaking, "a conquered country." The Moghal Empire having broken down, the sceptres of some of its component provinces were, in course of time, wrested from the incompetent hands which tried in vain to wield them; other Princes, with better titles, fortune, or judgment, held their seats, but submitted to control from the new paramount Power; in no case were any social organs that were capable of work ever set aside or destroyed. The new-comers, assuming this controlling power, founded their rule upon an inarticulate *plebiscitum*, expressed by silence, but none the less understood to be conditioned on faith and justice to be observed by them.

These considerations, far from diminishing the importance of Wellesley's policy, invest it with a special interest. We have already seen that his object was to assert the rights of his Government without infringing those of other States. At the beginning of the nineteenth century the rights of the British Government extended to the provinces which they had obtained by grant from the Emperor, or from his Vazir, the Nawab of Oudh. These they had to maintain, whether against Maratha, Muslim, or European foreigner. If Upper India had been left to itself it would have been a menace to the rest of the country, like a house on fire in the next street. While these anxieties were at their worst, the Governments of France and England broke off the Peace of Amiens, and Wellesley perceived the necessity of leaving nothing neglected that could protect the British Empire from the ambitious and unscrupulous Corsican who had made himself master of France. The splendour of Napoleon's genius and the pathos of his fall have combined to invest his name with a glamour that throws into the shade the figures of our brave ancestors who saved us and delivered Europe. But it is a fact that ought never to be forgotten, that for many a month transport lay in Boulogne harbour, and on the heights above stood a vast army eager to cross over to the shores held by those valiant but anxious sires of ours.

The Marquess Wellesley was one of the watchmen of the Empire, and it is impossible to read his despatches of that time without seeing that he thought, whether rightly or wrongly, that one of the defences of Dover was at Dehli. For a lucid summary of the British policy at that period, no better or clearer statement could be made than what is embodied in the review of the Governor-General's yet more famous brother, in Mr. Sydney Owen's *Selections from the Wellington Despatches*. About the same time a young traveller recorded in his diary an experience which befel him in marching through Orissa. A begging friar was found sitting by the way-side. "He spoke to us without any respect, . . . called us to him, but would not let us pass his boundary. When we were near, he said, 'Listen! When will you take this country? This country wants you: the Hindus are villains. When will you take the country?' We answered, 'Never.' He said, 'Yes! you will certainly take it.'"[1]

That little colloquy, which reminds us of Moira's record when in Oudh, expresses what must have been a very widespread feeling. So far back as 1761 we saw a Franco-Scot—the Chevalier Law—declaring to the Muslim historian that from Poona to Dehli he could find nothing deserving to be called a "government." But to

[1] Colebrooke's *Life of Mountstuart Elphinstone*, vol. i.

be governed is the first great need of an Asiatic who is not an absolute savage. Their very vocabularies show this: there is no word in any Asiatic idiom answering to "citizen"; the subjects are *raya* = protected.[1] The Indian subject will judge his ruler by this criterion; and the discriminating estimate of the modern Rulers of India supplied by a late eminent Russian journalist really conveys the highest commendation:—

"In reality the English have been the saviours of India. During whole centuries the history of India presents one continual spectacle of murder and devastation. The bloody era closes with the occupation of the country by the English, whose rule has been incomparably more mild, humane, and just than any government under which the Indians have ever lived."[2]

Whether the French, or the Russians themselves, would manage the country better, can only be dimly conjectured by those who have studied the cases of Central Asia under the one and North Africa under the other. To the natives, at least, the answer is unknown: and nothing is more terrible than the unknown for Asiatics. In any case the people of India cannot but gain by being reminded of the state of their country before the so-called "conquest."

But there is also a lesson to be learned by the ruling race; that an immigrant dominion can be preserved only by constant renewal of immigration. The social air of India is as degenerating to foreign virtue as her physical climate is relaxing to foreign strength. This truth holds through every department of life, and in all periods of Indian history. The breed of Indian horses is not maintained in beauty and vigour unless good sires and dams are imported from time to time. Without continual sowing of new seed, fruit and vegetables turn

[1] From the Arabic رعى, meaning "to protect." Hence the Anglo-Indian term "Ryot."

[2] Michael Katkoff, in the *Moscow Gazette*.

to weeds in the best tended gardens. We have seen how rapidly the Greeks in India decayed when communication with Europe was cut off. The same thing happened under the Moghal Empire. The men who followed Bābar from Turkestan were white men, with ruddy cheeks and fair hair ; a Spanish traveller, so late as the fourth generation after Bābar, noted the "rutilous" beauty of the Moghal ladies whom he met at a dinner-party ; "fairer," he said, in his high-flown Castilian way, "than any that the frigid Boreas engenders." The Moghal Emperors adopted the generous policy of employing native Muslim, and even Hindus, when they could find men of those classes fit for high command : yet they never failed to employ as many of these white immigrants from Central Asia and Persia as was at all possible. At length, after the reign of Mohammed Shah (who died in 1748) the Empire fell into confusion ; the Punjab became a cockpit for Sikhs and Afghans ; immigration ceased ; the Moghal State fell into the ruin we have seen—for want of fresh northern blood it perished of anæmia, even as the Manchu Empire in China seems to be doing now.

These facts by no means imply that native talent is not to be encouraged, or native valour and loyalty to be trusted. The trained regulars who conquered the brave Rājputs at Mairta and Sanganir ; the British sepoys who beat the regulars at Asai and destroyed the Sikh armies at Sabraon and Gujarat, were as good soldiers as those they vanquished ; but they were led by European officers. If the policy of Sindhia effected any cure of the Moghal anæmia, it was done by restoring the recourse to fresh blood for purposes of example and control : and surely no wise native of India can wonder if the British now adopt the principle that was forced on their own rulers. Ambaji and Begum Sombre would have made little show, either in war or in peace, without General de Boigne and his best officers ; it was their presence and their teaching that made the difference between Sindhia's regular sepoys and the Moghals of Ismail Beg or the Rāthors of Bijai Singh.

The superiority of most of the foreigners has been abundantly shown in the preceding chapters. In the first place there was the essential difference induced by *discipline*. It has been already pointed out that the native soldier was brave and faithful. We see for ourselves that he is so still. Put him behind a little cover, and he will skirmish or fire long shots all day. Inspire him with a point of honour and he will die in defence of his post—like the men of the 36th Sikhs at Saragarhi. Skinner illustrates this latter characteristic of the men of his day in a story that is very touching in its undecorated pathos. In 1804, after the war was over, but while dacoits and disbanded soldiers were still roaming about the country, he came with a British column to a fort which the commanding officer deemed it his duty to take. It was held by thirteen Rājputs, put in by some unnamed chieftain, but whom Skinner—who, as we have seen, was at that time full of native sympathy—persuaded to give up the place on his promise that they should not be disarmed. He brought them before the British commander, but this gentleman repudiated the clause and insisted on their weapons being left when they took their departure. The poor fellows appealed to Skinner, who warmly responded, while the Rājputs prostrated themselves in tears at his feet. "See, sir," said he, "I brought these men to you on an engagement which, as it appears, you are unable to ratify: I submit that we are, in that case, bound to put them back as they were; you can then take what course you think proper." The officer saw the justice of this plea; the Rājputs were allowed to march back to the fort with their arms; and they returned thither with expressions of joy: presently the British sent a storming party against them to scale the walls. The little garrison crouched behind their parapet until the stormers attained the wall; then each fired, and killed his man. A second body was at once sent forward, and met with the same fate. Finally, preparations being made for blowing open the gate with powder-bags, the Rājputs laid down their matchlocks, opened the gate, and received the third set of assailants sword in hand. When the fort was at last taken, the thirteen were found bayoneted in the gateway, with a mound of dead British sepoys lying around.

Such men were not cowards, though it is quite possible that, had the positions been reversed, the fort might never have been taken. The British sepoys who went up to the walls to be shot, or who fell round the desperate defenders in the gateway, were of the same blood and character; but they were disciplined men, each of whom knew that his comrades would obey orders without thought of what the consequence might be to himself; they would not have opened the gate without orders, which no skilled officer would have issued. *Science* in war is founded on genius informed by study, and only within the reach of a few; but the *art* of combat involves an unselfish neglect, and the habit of trusting to one's associates and to one's leader. The brave thirteen may have had neither the one nor the other; but each of them knew how to die fighting. This brings out the other point of distinction. However brave the Oriental soldiers may be (and the wars of the Russians against the Turks in Eastern Europe are enough to exemplify this), they must succumb—soon or late—to the inferior education, or the inferior character, of the officers who lead them. Men who are to prevail in war ought to be commanded by persons whom they can both trust and respect; who will set them examples of prolonged endurance and sustained enterprise in the face of all difficulties and sources of discouragement. These are qualities often found in Europeans because their ancestors have been free citizens, or—at least—have been accustomed to deal with events and institutions of a complicated nature. For that reason alone they are likely to win the regard and obedience of men descended from generations rendered torpid by the conditions of the stagnant and easy-going East. Thus the Sikhs, beaten by Thomas, attained supremacy over the Afghans when organised by Ventura and Avitabile, but were conquered by Bengal sepoys led by British officers and supported by British regiments ; the Sikhs, on their part, were good against any odds in Bengal sepoys when these conditions were reversed. These doctrines had been patent ever since the days of the *Anabasis*, for those who cared to observe and think for themselves ; they still awaited the demonstration of universal induction from the Indian wars of the eighteenth century and from the lives and characters of the adventurers as here set forth.

No one, however, could suppose that the employment of foreigners in positions of gain and honour was a natural usage, or that Sindhia and his imitators would have shown so much favour to Generals de Boigne and Perron if they could have found equally good subordinates among their own people. Arthur Wellesley recorded the opinion that these chiefs would have done better had they never entertained a European servant : but they, perhaps, knew their own business better even than he : in any case, what one did another had to do, on pain of ruin and destruction ; and, so long as British power held aloof, success attended the best use of the experiment. Those chiefs did best who employed the best officers, and under them a beginning of order appeared in the affairs of the community.

But, although civil administration may have shown some slight improvement where these adventurers had brought back peace to the troubled land, they were not—as we have seen—nearly so successful in that direction as they were in war ; and what has been said here is not to be applied without reservation to the practice of civil government. Here also there are certain qualities of energy and firmness which are best maintained by a constant renewal of the supply of officers from the governing country. Yet we ought surely to remember that some among the very greatest Indian administrators and statesmen have always been natives of India; from Sher Shah and Todar Mal down to the recent days of Sir Salar Jung and Sir T. Madhava Rao. Other qualifications are required for civil employ besides courage and initiative. Should it still seem good to any one to assert that the people are happier under the rule of the Native States than they are in British India, the means of disproof might not be easily found: although the British official might, no doubt, deny the assertion and shift from his own shoulders the burden of demonstration. One thing, at least, requires no argument: it is beyond the scope of controversy that these very Native States are defended, against each other and from foreign foes, only by the military strength of Great Britain based on the incomparable valour of British officers. Should it ever be proved that the bulk of the native population really do prefer the uncontrolled rule of Rajas and Nawabs, it may, perhaps, be said that their ideals are so hopelessly Bohemian as to forbid all prospect of civilising progress. But even so, the peace must be kept by military men who are alike superior to fear and to favour.

"During whole centuries," wrote the Moscow journalist already cited, "the history of India presents one continual spectacle of murder and devastation." The amendment of this has been the mission of Great Britain, though her agents may have originally gone out in search of trade alone. But the doctrine of "Hinterland" was even then pressing; and, in place of trade following the flag, it made the flag follow trade. Looking back on the conditions indicated in these pages, we can hardly imagine any other development possible.

EPILOGUE

Mr. Sidney Owen in his "Eve of the British Conquest" has endeavoured, not without success, to show the condition of the country in the eighteenth century, and to connect the episode with the History of British India.

The word "conquest" will convey to some readers an erroneous idea; for what took place at the end of this period was indeed rather in the nature of a deliverance.

In 1770 Hindustan was in a state of disintegration and misery: by the year 1820 unity and prosperity were close at hand. The work had been slow, but it would have been still slower had not Madhoji Sindhia and his European Agents prepared the ground by introducing the first principles of order and discipline. Wherever a railway or a canal mitigates the evils of dearth, wherever a peasant proprietor garners his crops in safety, there we see the effects of the Pax Britannica. But we must never withhold the credit due to those who, with very inferior resources, laid the foundation of what has since been completed. If, in the words of Virgil, day has returned to the East from us, it should be remembered that these men were, in a true sense, the harbingers of dawn.

Fuller details of the state of India at this period may be found in two or three works by the present writer, notably the monograph on Sindhia in "Rulers of India" Series, Oxford, 1892, and "History of India," Edinburgh, 1906, vol. i., chaps. ix., x., xi.

APPENDICES

APPENDIX I

A FEW details that could not well be fitted into our text may yet deserve record, as illustrative of the private affairs and personal fortune of some of the adventurers of the Anarchy. They are not of any special bearing on the state of India during that wild period; nevertheless those who have followed the main current of our narrative may care to know more about the persons who principally influenced its events.

The author is indebted for access to most of these sources of information to Mr. Stewart Sutherland, grandson of the Colonel Robert Sutherland of whom glimpses have been afforded in dealing with the career of General Perron. With Perron Sutherland was connected by marriage, having espoused the General's niece. Perron and the elder Hessing had found wives in the family of Derridon, still existing as small landed gentry near Agra;[1] and Mrs. Sutherland was daughter to Hessing and Anne Derridon, his wife, who remained in India when her sister, Madeleine, accompanied Perron to Europe, and became ancestress of several families of distinction in France.

Besides the land still held—or held within the last few years—by the Derridons (perhaps, originally, de Ridon), there are not many material monuments of the adventurers left in India. Amongst these few may be mentioned

[1] When the author was District Judge at Agra—1872–79—members of this family came as litigants into his court. They dressed like Europeans, but spoke Hindustani.

the tombs of the elder Hessing and Sutherland, with the church and palace built by Begum Sombre at Sardhana.

Hessing's tomb, in the Padretala (or Catholic Cemetery) of Agra, is a pretentious building of red sandstone, a copy of the famous Taj Mahal on a reduced scale. There is a long historical epitaph in English, giving a summary of the life and adventures of the deceased.

Sutherland's remains lie under a less assuming monument in a garden at Mathra which probably belonged to a residence of his now destroyed. Some small wreck of landed property remains, from the rent of which the maintenance of the tomb and garden is provided, the balance going to good works. This officer was a Scot of good birth, once an ensign in the Black Watch, who transferred himself to Sindhia's service and was made Brigade Major by General de Boigne and afterwards promoted to command a Brigade. He enjoyed the friendship and confidence of the General, as will be illustrated by some letters to be quoted hereafter. He had also the honour to co-operate with Colonel the Hon. A. Wellesley in 1800, and was in command at Agra when the fort was surrendered to Lake by the younger Hessing. Sutherland died soon after the peace.

The church and palace at Sardhana were built by the Begum a few years before her death in 1836, the architect being an Italian in her employ, Major Regholini. The house was inherited by the Begum's step-grandson, David Dyce, who took the name of Sombre and married the Hon. M. A. Jervis, daughter of the third Viscount St. Vincent. Mr. Dyce-Sombre dying in 1851, his widow married Lord Forester, and during her lifetime the house and grounds—seventy acres in all—were kept up. They have since been bought by the Vicar Apostolic of Agra, and are to become the site of a training college for young native missionaries. The palace is a fine building, standing on a basement 11 feet high. The front portico is approached by a vast flight of steps opening on a wide landing. A hall, 42 feet by 36 feet, leads to the various apartments, the private chambers of the Begum being entered by a winding staircase. Above all these and other bedrooms is the terraced roof so much affected in hot climates. The wings at the back, containing other apartments and offices, enclose a court-yard or small garden; and the front of the house is 160 feet in length. In the principal reception-rooms used to hang a number of portraits of the Begum's friends by Beechey, Melville, and other local artists—Sir David Ochterlony, on his white charger; General Cartwright; Baron Solaroli and Colonel J. R. Troup, husbands of Dyce-Sombre's sisters; Dyce-Sombre himself in a sort of Court-dress, with a Papal decoration. Amongst others was a small portrait-group, stiffly painted, representing the meeting of Lord Combermere and the Begum after the fall of Bhurtpur (1826). There were also half-lengths of Generals Ventura and Allard, the successors of Boigne and Perron, by whom the Sikh army was trained to fight the British in the middle of the nineteenth century. In the central hall was an ambitious piece, a life-size portrait of the Begum in advanced life, seated on a sort of throne and smoking her *hookah*. A well-painted head of a debauched-looking fellow in Moghal costume represented John, son of the famous George Thomas, who was brought up by the Begum and married to the daughter of an Armenian in her service, called Agha Wanus.[1] On issuing from the park gate one finds the road to the "Camera," or country house, occupied by the Begum until the completion of the above-described palace; and it was here that Bishop Heber was received by her in 1825, as described in his once well-known book.[2]

[1] These pictures are now in Government House, Allahabad; the portraits of the Begum by Melville being here reproduced by the courtesy of Sir James Digges La Touche.

[2] *Narrative of a Journey through the Upper Provinces of India, &c.*, 2 vols. 4to. London, 1828.

The Begum always maintained the position of an independent Princess, and showed hospitality to the military and civil officers of the neighbouring station of Meerut. There was a dinner-party every evening, at which Regholini, Colonel Dyce, the father of her subsequent heir, and the Reverend Father Scotti, the Chaplain, were usually present, along with their mistress; a band of music was in attendance, and the best wines of France and Spain circulated freely.

Such was the splendid termination of the slave-girl's career—a romance scarcely to be outdone by the most inventive fiction. When she felt the approach of death, she divested herself of all her property, by deed-of-gift in favour of young Dyce, subject to various important charges. The military fiefs were confiscated in consequence of her demise, the brigade being at the same time disbanded. Enough of the private and personal property was left to make a handsome provision of some £20,000 a year for the heir—which, indeed, ultimately proved the poor fellow's ruin. Very substantial benefactions were at the same time made to various religious bodies and undertakings.

The estates attached to the Sardhana fief were originally estimated to yield a revenue of Rx. 60,000 (six lakhs) per annum.[1] (The Rx., or conventional Indian £, was then worth over 20s.) On the Begum's death all but the park demesne were brought under the public fisc, which led to a long and costly litigation, terminated by an award to the effect that the confiscation was an act of public policy with which the courts were not at liberty to interfere.

It is a side-light on the state of the country in those days to learn that the British officials—as mentioned in the preceding text—at once reduced the assessments by 20 per cent. As the British of those days professed to take two-thirds to three-fourths of the net produce, we may find some difficulty in estimating what share may

[1] Afterwards increased by the Begum's assessments.

have been left to the Sardhana tenants. Cesses, transit-dues, and factory-taxes, to a considerable amount, were at the same time swept away. If this was the condition of a mediatised State, in the heart of the British territory, under a ruler of exceptional intelligence, desirous of standing well with the Government (and professing the Christian creed), what must have been the state of less fortunate districts before the introduction of British ideas and standards? In the year 1879, when the present writer was at Meerut, the land in Sardhana had largely increased its cultivated area, the assessment had fallen to an average of Rs. 2½ per acre, and wages had increased 150 per cent. over the rate current in the Begum's day. The five subdivisions are now among the most prosperous rural tracts in Hindustan.

The annexed table will show the pedigree of the late Mr. Dyce-Sombre, who—as will be seen—was not of kin to the Begum—

Walter Reinhardt, *al.* General Sombre;
m. a Mohammedan lady who survived
him and died a lunatic.
|
Aloysius Reinhardt, *al.* Nawab Zafar-
yab Khan, *m.* daughter of Colonel Lefèvre:
|
Anne Reinhardt, *al.* Sombre, *m.*
Mr. George Dyce, Agent to the Sardhana
Estates.
|
David Ochterlony Dyce-Sombre, *b.* 1808;
inherited the property, and *d.* with-
out issue, 1851; *m.* Hon. M. A. Jervis,
who *m.* (2nd) the late Cecil, Lord
Forester.

Of the church—called "Cathedral," though when the author knew the place there was no Bishop—there is not much to be said. Besides affording the unwonted spectacle of a large place of Christian worship in a Hindustan village, the building has no special claims to notice. It is, however, of respectable dimensions—170 feet long, with a central dome and two lofty spires at the east end: it was consecrated by the Vicar Apostolic in 1829. The interior is paved with marble and relieved by mouldings in hard stucco. In the back of the north transept is a group in white marble, by Tadolini of Rome, placed there by the gratitude of poor Dyce-Sombre. Pyramidal in form and exquisitely carved, it represents the deceased Princess seated on a platform surrounded by allegoric figures. Round the base stand life-size statues of civil and military officers; panels on the sides of the pedestal set forth the dates and deeds of the Begum's life, with historical groups in high relief commemorative of the Begum's court and camp.

APPENDIX II

BY the courtesy of the grandson of Colonel R. Sutherland, some interesting letters of General de Boigne have been consulted, which throw a new light upon the General's retirement from the service and return to Europe. The letters are written in a clear, bold hand; the English is perfectly intelligible though somewhat French in idiom. They cover a period of about nine months, viz., from the General's last movement on Lucknow to his embarkation at Calcutta.

The earliest bears date "Lucknow, 2nd April, 1796," and begins by expressing anxiety for news, as his correspondent must "be aware how interested I am in the successes and prosperity of our Prince"—Daulat Rao Sindhia, who was then, it may be noted, at peace with all his neighbours. The General then enters into some details about the administration of the force, and earnestly exhorts Sutherland to "be kind to every one of the officers, attentive to them as far as they deserve it, to give them their due, to promote in rank and pay those who may be entitled to it by their good services and merits, but discharge those from whom no good may be expected—better to have few good than many bad." He deals with the cases of officers who have been giving trouble and threatening to resign, and adds: "Detain nobody by force; every one has a right to be free and look out for himself; in doing so officers shall never be wanting, I hope to be able to provide the brigades with many." But he stops suddenly: "I will not decide nor interfere—*I have left the army*—on account of bad health, but not to plague myself about the details of the Service. I am, indeed, incapable of attending to any business." The letter ends with complaints of the writer's ill-health and probable intention of proceeding to sea under medical advice, adding an expression of confidence in Sutherland's "sagacity and judgment for all what concerns the good of the Prince and of his service."

From this conclusion, and from the entire omission of the name of Perron as his possible successor, it may perhaps seem to follow that the General regarded Sutherland as the future commander of the Regular Army. Had this happened, the whole course of subsequent events would have been affected to a degree which can only be conjectured. If Sindhia, under advice from a British officer, had complied with the policy of Lord Mornington, who can say if the authority of our nation would ever have been extended to Hindustan?

For many months General de Boigne lay at Lucknow in constant suffering and danger. Congestion of the liver and fever racked his frame and prevented him from taking an interest in the stirring events of which Lucknow was the scene. Sir John Shore, the British Governor-General, finding it impossible to wean the Nawab, Asaf-ud-daulah, from the life of frivolous debauchery under which he was rapidly sinking into the grave, resolved on trying the effect of a personal interview; but the letters contain no mention of his visit. The only concern of the invalid is for his old master and comrades, mixed with a creditable solicitude for the two daughters whom he had, it seems, left at Aligurh. "Protect and defend them," he implores his friend; "and support my interest in everything in which your assistance may be required." A landed estate in what is now the Etah District had been assigned for the support of the girls; but the anxious father intended to return as soon as he was restored to health. If he should have to go to Europe—"which I hope may not be the case—it would not take me more than eighteen months; knowing that Europe will (not) nor ever can suit my temper nor constitution. . . . Be happy!" he ends, "and believe me for ever, etc."

The next letter is dated the 1st September; the rainy season was ending and the most trying part of the Indian year at hand. But the sick man does not mend: his "illness has been so great for these several months past that I thought it was all over for me . . . inconceivable how severe have been my sufferings. . . . God be praised! all is for the best." He writes a long letter: this one has more than 1,000 words, all thoughtful and wise. In spite of the declaration of April that he has left the army, his plan of a sea-voyage is only to go round from Calcutta to Bombay, there to join "the Prince" at Poona, and return to "Indostan" with the 1st Brigade. "Nothing could give me greater pleasure than to hear of the successes and prosperity of the Brigades raised by me and which give bread to one hundred thousand souls at least." Sutherland is exhorted to "conquer his hostility towards the Mohammedan Paymaster, and warned that it is the Hindoos, and not the Prophet's followers, who are the real foes of Europeans in India." Other advice and suggestions follow, but nothing like interference; compliments to Lakwa Dada, the Brahman Minister, soon to fall from power and end his days in exile: and the long epistle ends with remembrances to the officers "and all the Men of the Army: it will be agreeable to them to see though yet far from them I have them yet in remembrance."

On the 13th, the General writes again, "having not for these six months past enjoyed a single moment of good health," he has incurred the reproaches of his friends for not answering their letters; but he has now a new and much-esteemed medical adviser, Dr. Hare, who gives good hope of recovery when the cold season has had its healing effect: "if he can prevent my getting worse before the end of October." He has heard from Lakwa Dada, to whom he begs Sutherland to announce his intention of writing soon. "Tell him all accounts are to be delivered; at my departure it was so ordered in General Orders: so long I am alive I have nothing at all to do with accounts, it is the business of the Mahratta Chief." Once more Sutherland is exhorted to be reconciled to the Muslim Paymaster: "it is better to have him for friend than for enemy; if you know your own interest you will follow my advice." He is sorry to hear that Mr. Dawes has left the service to plant indigo; this is a falling industry; he gives details, adding that he himself has lost "four lakhs rupees," but is too ill to care. (Dawes returned to the service, and died fighting in the battle near Poona where Holkar defeated Sindhia, 25th October, 1802.) The General ends with saying that he gets the Poona news from the *Bombay Gazette*, and telling his correspondent to "be happy and successful."

On the 7th January, 1797, the General writes from Calcutta—before leaving Lucknow he had been mending, but the damp cold of a Bengal winter has brought a relapse: "Few men can have suffered more than I have this year past, particularly since my arrival to Bangala." He has taken his passage "both for Bombay and the Cape of Good Hope . . . if I am so fortunate to recover my health, I shall proceed immediately to Poona to join the 1st Brigade and meet the Prince; if I remain as I am, I am obliged to go to the Cape; then it will be six or seven months before I can be back to Coel, which God forbid it should be the case! . . . Let me proceed to Poona or to the Cape. I trust and most warmly recommend you to continue your attachment, as you have done till now, to the Prince, to the good of the service, and indeed to maintain the fame and credit we have obtained at the sacrifice of so much blood and so much fatigue." In all which we may, if we please, observe either an actual commander, fully intending to resume his duties after a brief convalescence, or a man who knows that his health is gone, and who bids farewell to the scene of his labour, but "casts a longing, lingering look behind." Of the reality of the General's breakdown one can hardly doubt; in this very letter he says he would give up all his wealth—considerable as we know it to have been—if he could emerge from a state of suffering to which, as he quaintly says, "death is a thousand times as preferable." He proceeds to give some instructions about the Etah estate—"my Jaghire in the Province of Jalleyssore"—and to commend to Sutherland's protection "my women, my reputation, and all that concerns me: if you have gratitude you will prove it; I will say no more." General Martin will represent him as his general agent, and will always know his address and forward letters. The letter ends with instructions on behalf of the "weadows of officers"; and the protection of "about nine country-born young men, sons of officers," to whom ensigns' commissions have been promised "at Rs. 125 per month, and when Perron comes, give him some." By this time the General, perhaps, knew who was to be his successor; but he sends him no greeting, implying—it may be—that Perron and Sutherland were not friends.

The last letters of the series are dated on January 15th, and written on board ship, to be posted doubtless by the Hugli pilot on leaving at the Sandheads. The General now speaks plainly as to his intention "to go no farther than Bombay, and proceed thence to Poona; in the end to pay my respects to the Prince . . . but if I am doomed to remain in my present state I shall be obliged to proceed to the Cape at the advice of the Doctors and at the solicitations of my friends . . . as for Europe, I don't think of it, but as a last resource, well aware that a single winter (there) would kill me, so much have I been worst since the cold has begun in Bangala." The European winter, as it turned out, was to prove a different thing from a Calcutta cold season; and nearly thirty years of honour and usefulness awaited the veteran in that Europe which he seemed to regard with so much anxiety: "to live a single year in Europe would be my death:" if the Cape does not restore him, yet, "God be praised! farther can't at the moment think of any place of safety in Europe, to which adding that it being now twenty-seven years (since) I left for the last time my native place, I have not a relation or person of my acquaintance (left there)." He cannot therefore look forward to the influence and power to which he has become accustomed, "with the advantage of being able to do good to numbers of people." Had all this—so contrary to the ultimate result—been only addressed to Sindhia and other natives of India, we might be tempted to regard it as a *placebo* to cover desertion. But it being repeatedly urged so earnestly upon a European comrade, and always in company with marks of unremitting sympathy with the service, we are surely justified in believing that, to the last, the writer hoped to resume his command in India. But there is equal reason to believe that the General did not leave the Marathas with much regret, whatever may have been his feelings towards "the Prince" or his European servants. In this very letter he returns to the subject of the Hindus and their irreconcilable enmity for Europeans. "Believe me," he says, "and be assured all the Mahratta Chiefs are our mortal enemies, as well as the Pandetts" (the Brahmans), "and it is not one of them that would not see with the greatest pleasure the extinction of the Brigades; to effect that purpose nothing better than by our losing the Provinces." The gallant officer is led by haste into a tangle of words; the meaning is clear enough: the Lakwa Dadas, Ambajis, &c., would gladly see their master expelled from Hindustan if the event should lead him to dispense with his regular force and European officers. Therefore he adds, to Sutherland, a caution that "it behoves you to have a vigilant eye to the entire preservation of both; your own interest and the good of thousands depend on it!" These reflections and instructions are not only of use in showing the opinion entertained by the retiring commander as to the situation of his correspondent, but they throw some light on the subsequent policy and conduct of General Perron.

Before concluding this letter of farewell, the writer once more earnestly commends to Sutherland the interests of the Prince and of the service: "to maintain the reputation of the troops under your command requires activity and exactitude in every part . . . as you are wise, I flatter myself to find things on my return in good order. I shall say no more; write to me every three or four months." In a separate letter of the same date, sent through Colonel Martin, the General implores Sutherland to take charge of the Jalesar *jaigir*, remembering that it is not a military fief but a freehold from the late Mahadaji's favour under the seal manual of the Empire (*Al-Tamgha*); so that it may be secured against "the rapacity" of Marathas and Pandits. The income is to be "the patrimony of my children till they are of age, the maintenance of my two girls . . . their pension being attached and affixed on the said Jaghir."

Whether the young ladies lived to enjoy the provision thus made for them; whether Sutherland looked after their settlement in life; and whether they left any descendants of the great Savoyard General, it is now too late to ascertain. It is only clear that General de Boigne had confidence in Sutherland, who doubtless justified that trust for the rest of his brief career.

Vain conjectures have been already expressed as to the possible variation in events had Sindhia regarded

Sutherland with the eyes of his departed General. He preferred to trust the Frenchman, with the result that we know. Perron intrigued and vacillated, almost to the last; his officers deserted or betrayed him; and he esteemed himself lucky to escape with his goods to the protection of a generous foe. The last of the letters kindly supplied by Mr. Sutherland shows Perron in the act of withdrawing his property from the fort at Agra, under a pass from Colonel R. Ball, commanding for Lake at Sasni. It is addressed to George Hessing, and dated September 15, 1803. The English is irreproachable.

Amongst other letters due to the courtesy of Mr. Sutherland, not the least interesting are those addressed to his grandfather by the future Duke of Wellington when the latter was conducting operations in the valley of the Kistna in 1800. It was the year after the fall of Tippu, Sultan of Mysore; and Arthur Wellesley—as he then was—had taken the field against one of Tippu's former followers—locally known as "Dhundia Waugh"—who had escaped from Seringapatam and attempted to live on the country at the head of a band of freebooters. Wellesley had pushed the robbers across the country into Dharwar, and now found reason to hope that he might bring them to bay. But to do this effectually he required the aid of Sindhia, whose forces were then in the Deccan. The first letter on the subject bears date, "Camp on the right bank of the Malprabha, August 13th, 1800." It begins, in the most direct fashion, by referring to information which must have reached the correspondent from the Court of Poona, and to the success which has hitherto attended the British troops. "This being the case," proceeds the young Brigadier, "and having besides received intelligence from Lieutenant-Colonel Palmer that Dowlut Row Scindiah (*sic*) had informed him that his troops could co-operate with me, I am induced to write to you. Doondiah Waug is now on the south bank of the (Gulperba ?)[1] river; his object is evidently to cross it and to avoid the troops under my command. It is in your power to prevent this, and thus to render an important service to the Peshwa and his allies. As I understand you are an Englishman, I address you in English, and I shall be obliged if you will let me know what steps you intend to take with a view to compliance with the wish when I have an opportunity of mentioning your services to the British Government and to that of Poona.

"I have the honour to be, Sir, with respect,

"Your most obedient, humble servant,

"ARTHUR WELLESLY.

"To the Officer Commanding the
forces of Dowlut Row Scindiah."

This letter appears to have been a fortnight on the road; on the 2nd September it must have been received by Sutherland at Poona, for on that date he wrote to the Colonel informing him that he had communicated the contents to his subordinate, Captain Brownrigg, directing him to place himself under Colonel Wellesley's orders on condition of his not taking his detachment beyond the limits of the Maratha territory. "Give me leave to assure you," added Sutherland, "that though circumstances have placed me under the direction of a native Prince, I still consider myself bound by every principle of honour . . . to watch for every opportunity of rendering service to my fellow-countrymen . . ." These professions were handsomely acknowledged by Wellesley, who added that if the enemy "should return into the Mahratta country their services would certainly be availed of. And," proceeds the writer, "I shall take the opportunity of stating to Captain Brownrigg my opinion of the manner in which the troops under his orders can be

[1] Perhaps the Ghatprahba, an affluent of the Kistna, which breaks from the mountains near Gokak.

employed [so as] to render most service to the common cause. The correspondence would be forwarded to the Government of Fort St. George; and the Colonel had no doubt but that the Right Honourable the Governor [Lord Clive] would derive the greatest satisfaction from perusal." This letter is dated from camp, September 7th. On the 20th of the same month Wellesley gives Brownrigg the following laconic account of the end of the operations against Dhundia: "I fell in with his army on the 10th instant, and an action ensued in which his troops were entirely defeated and he was killed." This action was fought at Manoli.

The remaining letters are formal—one from Brownrigg offering congratulations, and one from the Colonel in courteous acknowledgment. It is only needful to add that after the conclusion of the war, four years later, Brownrigg was allowed to enter the service of the Honourable East India Company, in which he lost his life, being killed at the siege of Sirsa (presumably in 1818).[1]

An interesting account of some of the adventurers was published by Mr. Fisher Unwin some years ago, the author being the late Mr. Herbert Compton.. There is no date on the title-page, but the work was noticed in the *Indian Magazine and Review* for December, 1892. The title is *A Particular Account of the European Military Adventurers of Hindustan*; but the only full memoirs are those of Boigne, Perron, and Thomas, the rest being collectively dealt with in an Appendix.

[1] *Vide Imperial Gazetteer of India*, xiii. 12.

APPENDIX III

THE following announcement appeared in the *Homeward Mail* of August 12, 1899 :—

"The death is announced, at his residence near Etah, of the fourth Lord Gardner. He claimed to be descended through his mother from the Imperial House of Dehli. The late Lord Gardner had never left India, but was content to live the life of an ordinary zemindar on his estate. Lord Gardner, who held a title in the peerage of Ireland (1800), as well as in that of England (1806), which carries a seat in the House of Lords, but never formally proved his right, leaves a son, a minor, who now succeeds *de jure* as fifth Baron. The late peer had also a brother resident in Oude, and there are numerous cousins in England descended from the first lord.

"Few noble families can have had a stranger history or present a stronger illustration of the futility of social distinctions."

INDEX